Daily
INSPIRATION
Thru God's Word

SHARE SOME
LOVE
House of Prayer
Evangelistic Ministries Inc.

MOSES JOHNSON SR. &
VIVIAN M. JOHNSON

WESTBOW·
PRESS
A DIVISION OF THOMAS NELSON
& ZONDERVAN

WestBow Press books may be ordered through booksellers or by contacting:

WestBow Press
A Division of Thomas Nelson & Zondervan
1663 Liberty Drive
Bloomington, IN 47403
www.westbowpress.com
1 (866) 928-1240

ISBN: 978-1-4908-4368-1 (sc)
ISBN: 978-1-4908-4370-4 (hc)
ISBN: 978-1-4908-4369-8 (e)

Library of Congress Control Number: 2014912194

Printed in the United States of America.

WestBow Press rev. date: 07/17/2014

Dedication

We dedicate this devotional first and foremost to our Lord and Savior Jesus Christ without whom this would never be a success. Thank You Lord for Your plans & Your purpose for our lives. You have blessed us to be a blessing. Lord, we pray You will get ALL THE GLORY from the birthing of this book.

We dedicate our first book to our children: Kameisha, Janeal, Shauna, Natalia, Kwayne, Akeam, Moses Jr. and all nine grandchildren. Each one of you inspired thoughts that kept us putting pen to paper and making keystrokes on our computer day and night. We love you and thank God for you. May the Lord continue to do great things in your lives. We also dedicate this book to our parents: Rev. Dr. Frances W. Mackey and In Loving Memory of the late Rev. Dr. Arthur L. Mackey Sr. (Vivian's parents), In Loving Memory of: Ms. Murna Lane & Mr. Alphonso Johnson (Moses' Parents)

And we know that all things work together for good to them that love God, to those who are the called according to His purpose.
– Romans 8:28

For I know the plans I have for you, declares the LORD, plans to prosper you and not to harm you, plans to give you hope and a future.
– Jeremiah 29:11

And the LORD answered me, and said, Write the vision, and make *it* plain upon tables, that he may run that readeth it.
– Habakkuk 2:2

Acknowledgements

We are grateful to so many people who encouraged us in one way or another to take this project from a dream to reality.

We are thankful to Ms. Delrose MacDonald who encouraged us many steps along the way with the rich life and legacy she displays in "conversation" with us over the years. Mrs. Merlena Stewart and Mrs. Angela Williams are two towers of inspiration and strength whom God placed in our lives to inspire and strengthen us from start to finish on this project.

We acknowledge the late Rev. Dr. Arthur L. Mackey Sr. and Rev. Dr. Frances W. Mackey for influencing our lives in such a mighty way. Taking the time to pour into us personally and tremendously. Without you both this would never have materialized. We thank God for you and your input in our lives.

Rev. Arthur L. Mackey Sr. & Elder Brenda Mackey, Pastor and Pastors' wife of the Mt. Sinai Baptist Church Cathedral in Roosevelt, New York. Pastor Mackey as an author of many books yourself we thank you for your input on this project. Thank you both for pouring leadership into us.

Pastor Tyrone Woodside and Pastor Frances Woodside, Perfecting Love Church in Winter Haven, Florida. Thank you both for all of your love, prayers and continued support of our family.

The Womack Family – We love you and thank God for you. Bishop J. Raymond Mackey and the Tabernacle of Joy Church, thank you all very much. To all of our aunts, uncles, brothers, sisters, nieces, nephews, cousins, family and extended family we love you and thank God for you.

To our many friends and everyone else involved indirectly we appreciate all you have done to help us and to bless us. To our Facebook friends and those who participate in the "Share Some Love House of Prayer Evangelistic Ministries Group." You all were essential in helping us to make this a success.

Thank you to everyone at Westbow Press for your prayers, patience, assistance and professional guidance.

Prayer

Father, we thank you for bringing this book to pass.
It has been a long journey. Thank You Lord! We made it!
Bless each person reading this book we pray.

Save, heal, deliver, set-free, draw souls closer to You Lord.
Enlighten, encourage and strengthen the reader.
In Jesus name we pray. Amen.

Trust in the LORD with all thine heart;
and lean not unto thine own understanding.
In all thy ways acknowledge him,
and he shall direct thy paths.
– Proverbs 3:5,6

Introduction

The format for these devotions were chosen with great care and we suggest that, to get the maximum satisfaction from each devotion each day you take time to really absorb and/or meditate on each devotion.

As you read each day's subject, think about what it means to you. Then meditate in the scripture passage for a moment (most scriptures are from the New King James Version of The Holy Bible taken from: http://www.biblegateway.com/versions/ and then delve into the body which keeps with the theme or the subject of the devotion for that day. Pray the prayer earnestly and even add as the Holy Spirit leads. When you get to the encouragement section take some time to think about it as you read and even paraphrase or build on the statement there encouraging you for that particular day. The process should take five to fifteen minutes. Depending on the time you have for your devotion. However, ensure to have some time set aside each day to devote to our God where we can spend it with Him and benefit greatly from our devotion daily. We believe in the power of prayer. God has made us to be "Encouragers of One Another". God still answers prayer. He has done so much for us we cannot tell it all. We thank God for what He has done, we look forward to the future and the great things He has in store. For your glory Lord! Yes, for Your glory!!! May God bless you! Enjoy your daily spiritual food from God's hands through His humble servants,

Elder Moses & Elder Vivian Johnson

Contents

Whom He Foreknew

For whom He foreknew, He also predestined to be conformed to the
image of His Son, that He might be the firstborn among many brethren.
Moreover whom He predestined, these He also called; whom He called,
these He also justified; and whom He justified, these He also glorified.
– Romans 8:29-30

According to God's teaching to His followers, which is also
a revelation of the mysteries of His kingdom to his believers
or followers or children, it doesn't matter what you may have
done in your life and how you see yourself as a result, God
can make something wonderful out of your past. He is never
surprised by anything we do or have done. He knew all that
would happen in our lives before we came here. He knew our
beginning, our ending and everything in between that would
take place on this earth before we were even formed in our
mother's womb. Therefore He had a plan for each person's life
according to the decisions we would make and the rewards
or consequences we would incur as a result of these choices.
He knew just how to continue the conscientious life or fix the
messed up ones when they both accepted His calling. Here's
an even greater mystery. He knew us even before we were
formed in our mother's womb (see Jeremiah 1:5-6). Thank You
Lord. You knew the life each individual who would eventually
answer Your call would live, and You planned for each
individual's life accordingly. Whom you foreknew, you truly
predestined to be conformed to the image of Your Son, Jesus
Christ, that He might be the firstborn among many brethren.
You who began a good work in all of us Your children, is
faithful to complete it.

Prayer and Encouragement

Thank You Lord for Your plan for each and every
one of us Your children. You never fail.

Trust in the Lord with all your heart,
and lean not on your own understanding.
In all your ways acknowledge Him, and
He shall direct your paths.
– Proverbs 3:5-6

It's a Bright & Beautiful Day

To appoint unto them that mourn in Zion, to give unto them
beauty for ashes, the oil of joy for mourning, the garment of
praise for the spirit of heaviness; that they might be called
trees of righteousness, the planting of the LORD,
that He might be glorified.
– Isaiah 61:3

It's a brand new day. Let's make it the best day of our life,
ever!!! Praise the Lord everyone!!! Yes, let the people praise
Him! Let us give our God the highest praise!
Hallelujah!!!!

Prayer & Encouragement

Lord, from the rising of the sun until the going down of
the same, Your name is worthy to be praised. We give You
all the praise!!!! We give You the highest praise!!!!!
Hallelujah!!!!

Never stop praising Our God.
There is none like Him in the entire universe and He dwells
(Inhabits or lives) in the praises of His people.
Awesome!!!!!!!!!

We Have the Victory!!!

The parable of the prodigal son outlines the victory for the two sides in the church. On one side is the prodigal group that lived their lives riotously out in the world and finally came to their senses and gave God their hearts. On the other side is the group that lived their entire life in the church never venturing outside to see or experience what this sinful and adulterous world has to offer.

Our Father knows that both need to be saved because not just some but all have sinned (Romans 3:23) and all deserve death (Romans 6:23). Therefore He saves both sides. It's a great victory for our Father, like the songwriter says...

I heard an old, old story, How a Savior came from glory,
How He gave His life on Calvary to save a wretch like me;
I heard about His groaning, of His precious blood's atoning,
Then I repented of my sins and won the victory.

Jesus paid it all for us and all to Him we owe.

Sin had truly left a crimson stain
But He washed us white as snow.

Prayer and Encouragement

Thank You Lord for Your indescribable gift of eternal life through Jesus Christ Our Lord. Romans 6:23b. Amen.
We all need the Savior, regardless of the life we've lived.

Have the Mind of Christ

Let this mind be in you which was also in Christ Jesus.
– Philippians 2:5

If there is any consolation in Christ, if any comfort of love, if any fellowship of the Spirit, if any affection and mercy, fulfill His joy by being like-minded having the same love, being of one accord, of one mind. Let nothing be done through selfish ambition or conceit, but in lowliness of mind let each esteem others better than himself. May each person look out not only for his own interest, but also for the interest of others. Each time we're confronted with a decision to make, we should ask ourselves, "What would Jesus do?" Then do just what we know Jesus would do. Let this mind be in you that was also in Christ Jesus, who, being in the form of God did not consider it robbery to be equal with God, but made himself of no reputation, taking the form of a bondservant, and coming in the likeness of men. He humbled Himself and became obedient to the point of death even the death of the cross. Therefore God has highly exalted Him and given Him the name which is above every name, that at the name of Jesus, every knee will bow, of those in heaven, and of those on earth, and of those under the earth, and that every tongue will confess that Jesus Christ is Lord to the glory of God the Father. Humble yourselves under the mighty hand of God, and He will exalt you in due season.

Prayer & Encouragement

Lord teach us how to have the mind of Jesus Christ. Teach us Lord to renew our minds daily through Your Word. Amen. To have the mind of Jesus Christ, start with humility.

What God Requires of Us

Assuredly, I say to you, inasmuch as you did it to one
of the least of these My brethren, you did it to Me.
– Matthew 25:40

Jesus in this text points out the criterion by which we will be judged: our treatment of those who are hungry, homeless, poor, diseased, and imprisoned (Matt. 25:37-39). Here Jesus equates our treatment of those who are destitute or distressed with our treatment of Himself. What we do for others, we do for Jesus. Mother Theresa was the perfect example of Jesus' lecture here. We must never be too busy to help someone on our life's journey. The songwriter said, "If I could help somebody as I travel along, then my living shall not be in vain." Our late Pastor Arthur Mackey Sr.'s favorite expression was, "As long as the breath of God is in this body, I must do the work of Him who sent me. I must rescue the perishing, and care for the dying. I cannot sit idle while the souls of men are dying daily." And he lived those words each day. I know, because I was with him every step of the way as he mentored me to become a minister of the gospel of Jesus Christ. Unless we live this life the way Jesus instructs us to, we will have lived our lives most miserably. When we come to the end of our journey and stand before the LORD, we don't want to hear, "Depart from me for I never knew you." Obey the Lord in all things so you can hear Him say, "Well done good and faithful servant, you have been faithful in a little. Come on up higher so I can make you ruler over much."

Prayer and Encouragement

LORD help us to be obedient to you in all things we pray.
No matter how it looks, obey the LORD in all things.
The reward is well worth it all.

6

My Life Is In Your Hands

In Your book they all were written, the days fashioned
for me, when as yet there were none of them.
– Psalm. 139:16

What a comfort to know that while our future may sometimes look unclear at best, and futile at worst, God knows precisely what lies ahead. The disastrous things that come to us in life are the result of fallen humanity living on a broken planet.

Through it all, God's hand is still
steady and He will lead us.

Prayer and Encouragement

God in accordance with Your Word, we pray that we
will beware, lest there be in us an evil heart of unbelief in
departing from You, living God. We pray that we will exhort
ourselves daily, while it is called "today," lest we be hardened
through the deceitfulness of sin.
– Hebrews 3:12-13
Amen!!!

When you carry a Bible, the devil gets a headache.
When you open it, he collapses. When he sees you reading it,
he faints. When he sees you living it, he flees. He will try his
best to discourage you but when you do all these things,
he will be defeated. I just defeated him.

7

His Plan and Purpose for Us

For I know the thoughts that I think toward you, says the Lord,
thoughts of peace and not of evil, to give you a future and a hope.
– Jeremiah 29:11

Many people set goals for themselves which includes resolutions for their family, job, church attendance and involvement and other interests. While this may be a positive intention many never get started on these endeavors while most who do get started never go through to the end. The most important thing to do each New Year is find out what God's plans are for us and try our best to live our lives according to His purpose. We know that from Jeremiah chapter 29 and verse 11 God knows the plan He has for us. He knows the thoughts He thinks toward us which are thoughts of peace and not of evil. To give us a bright future and hope. He is omniscient and therefore knows our beginning to our end. Our future is in His hands or His control. So we need not busy ourselves with unnecessary plans. A man's heart plans his ways but the Lord directs His steps. This is the conclusion of the whole matter. Love and obey God. Will to do His will, thereby allowing God to carry out His plan and so you will be happy and He will be well pleased with you.

Prayer and Encouragement

Lord in this coming year we want our new year's resolution
to be in line with Your plans for us. Please lead us to
be obedient to You and fulfill Your purpose for us.
Will to do God's will and everything will fall in place.

Encourage Yourself

God says in His word-
'Fear not, for I *am* with you;
Be not dismayed, for I *am* your God.
I will strengthen you,
Yes, I will help you, I will uphold you
with My righteous right hand.'
– Isaiah 41:10

Prayer and Encouragement

Father while listening to those You may use to correct
and encourage us, help us to stay focused on You and to
encourage ourselves in You Lord. Grant us wisdom to know
and accept when you're using our brother or sister
to speak into our lives Lord. Amen.

It doesn't matter who you are or what you've done. God knew
you before you came into existence and knows your every
fault and every failure. He already planned for every mishap
and every major failure in each person's life. He never fails
and if you will allow Him He will overpower
the enemy and deliver you, ultimately.

Glory to God! Hallelujah!!!

Trust and Obey

You will keep him in perfect peace, whose mind
is stayed on You. Because he trusts in You
– Isaiah 26:3.

The Bible tells us in Proverbs 3:5-6. "Trust in the Lord with all your heart and lean not unto your own understanding. In all your ways acknowledge Him, and He shall direct your path." When you love a person you will trust that person. Sometimes such friendship turns out "good" even with a few "bumps" here and there. But overall you'll say it was a "good" relationship. With God there is no let downs on His part. Keep your mind on Him and He'll keep you in perfect peace because you trust Him. That trust in Him is with all your heart and there's no more leaning on your own understanding. In all your ways you acknowledge Him and He'll direct your path. It is a path He's been down before. A path He's taken many times before you. A path that may be dark and dreary but you're sure to finish the journey successfully. Because you know the God whom you serve. He will never leave you comfortless. He will never leave you nor forsake you. The journey He started you on, He will be right there with you until the end. He knows the plans He has for you. Plans of a bright future and a hope. Plans of an expected end. Just put your hands in His and He'll do the rest. He'll see you all the way through to the end.

Prayer & Encouragement

God we thank you that even though there's a thief who wants to steal, kill and destroy us, we have a way of escape through

You, who came to give us abundant life in
this present age and eternal life in our future.

Isn't it sweet, the plans our God has for us?
It starts with us accepting, believing and
trusting in Him. Then keep our minds on Him
and letting him direct our path.

Rejoice In the Lord Always

Rejoice in the Lord always and again I say rejoice.
– Philippians 4:4

Rejoice, our Savior is risen. Rejoice, it is finished. Rejoice, it's the end of the conflict. Rejoice, the battle is over and Jesus is Lord of all. Rejoice, rejoice, rejoice and again I say rejoice. Jesus you reign supreme. You are Lord and God of all. You reign forever and ever. Amen. Lord do you remember when You walked among men? You know if You are looking below, its worse now than then. Cheating and stealing, violence and crime. Lord teach us how to rejoice in times like these. Knowing that the victory is already won by You. With divine wisdom from you we will be fighting victory instead of battles. You know Lord, I once thought number one would be me in this world. I thought I could make it on my own. But I came to realize that I cannot do this without You. Without You I am nothing. Without You I can do nothing. But I can do all things through You, Jesus Christ, who strengthens me. I therefore encourage everyone for this reason to rejoice in the Lord always and again I say rejoice.

Prayer & Encouragement

Teach us to rejoice in You always. Please Lord. Lord, give us the true joy that only comes from having Your presence in our lives daily. You're on the Lord's side, rejoice in Him always and again I say rejoice because you're on the winning team.

Our God Supplies All Our Needs

I've been young and now am old, yet I've not seen the
righteous forsaken, nor his descendants begging bread.
– Psalm 37:25

Jehovah Jireh is one of our God's names among many others.
Jehovah Jireh means the LORD will provide. As His name
suggests so He is. Not one of His Saints has ever been forsaken
and the generations of His Saints have never had to go begging.
Our God will provide. Only trust Him. Jehovah Nissi means
God is our Banner; Jehovah Ropha means He is our Healer;
Jehovah Roe, He sees; Jehovah Rohi, He is our Shepherd;
Jehovah Shama, He is there; Jehovah Shaloam, He is our Peace;
Jehovah Tsidkeno, He is our righteousness.

These are only a few of God's names
and when He declares I AM WHO I AM,
He's saying to all creation, I will be whatever or whomever
you want me to be, I will meet your every need in whatever
way you need them to be met.

Our God is an awesome God.
Is there anything too hard for Him?
Is His Hand too short to bless? Never!

Our God reigns supreme over the entire universe. Not just
Africa. Not just Asia. Not just North or South America. Not just
Europe or Australia or Antarctica or any place else on earth. He
reigns over the planet Earth and Mercury, Venus, Mars, Jupiter,
Saturn Uranus, Neptune, and Pluto. He reigns over everywhere
in this galaxy and ALL other galaxies and beyond. He reigns
over the natural realm and the spirit realm.

He reigns everywhere, forever and ever and ever and beyond all that. How can a God as our God, the only true and living God with such wisdom and power let one of His Saints whom He has such abounding love for be forsaken or His descendants go begging bread?

Prayer & Encouragement

Father, we thank you for loving and caring for us,
man whom you made a little bit lower that angels.
Thank you for being mindful of us Father and taking the time
to make us so special in Your sight. Amen.

The next time you feel like there's too much going on in
"your" world and you feel like giving up, remember that Your
Great and Almighty God will never forsake His own nor will
He let you or your descendants go begging bread.
He values you too much to let anything above which you
can handle happen to you and He ALWAYS provides
a way of escape through it all. God Bless You!!!

Never Give Up (Don't Quit)

Therefore my beloved brethren, be steadfast, immoveable,
always abounding in the work of the Lord,
knowing that your labor is not in vain in the Lord.
– 1 Corinthians 15:58

People who persevere
usually succeed at the point
where others give up.

At that point where you feel like giving up could be the moment your breakthrough is about to happen. No matter the challenge or opposition you're up against never give up while working for the Lord. In addition to Paul's statement in 1 Corinthians 15:58 above, in his second letter to the Corinthian church he says, "Our light affliction which is but for a moment is working for us a far more exceeding and eternal weight of glory." (2 Corinthians 4:17). Again Paul says in Romans 8:18, "I consider that the sufferings of this present time are not worthy to be compared with the glory which shall be revealed in us." Never give up. I know from past experience that sometimes these words seem to mean nothing when we're in the midst of some fiery trial but just hold on and stay in prayer even when there seems to be no clarity in the situation or you just cannot understand. Remember the cloud of witnesses in Hebrews 12:1 (Therefore seeing we are surrounded by such a great cloud of witnesses, let us lay aside every weight and the sin which so easily ensnares us, and let us run with endurance the race that is set before us). Encourage yourself in the Lord by telling yourself, if they made it I can make it too.

Winston Churchill said the nose of the bull dog is slanted backwards so he doesn't have to let go and Evangelist Marilyn

Hickey wrote a book on the theme "Having Bulldog Faith." We need to adopt that "Bulldog Faith" on this journey. I know sometimes even the people you're looking up to in the Kingdom of God will sometimes let you down. Sometimes their actions seem to be saying they don't want you around them. That's ok, Jesus didn't save you to serve anyone else as Lord but Him. Humble yourself keep on praying for everyone in the kingdom and remain steadfast, immoveable, always abounding in the work of the Lord even when you're called everything except the child of God you know for sure you are, because He called you His child.

It's not what people call you,
it's who God calls you
that is important.

Prayer & Encouragement

Father give us that bulldog faith we need to persevere at times when we feel like throwing in the towel. For we know the loving, merciful, kind, gracious and compassionate God you are Who has only excellent and perfect things in store for us when we hold on until the fullness of time comes according to your plan and purpose for us. Thank You Lord. Amen!!! Hold on. No matter what the circumstance God is faithful to deliver His promise.

Be Careful Where You Venture

Be sober, be vigilant; because your adversary the devil walks
about like a roaring lion, seeking whom he may devour. Resist
him, steadfast in the faith, knowing that the same sufferings
are experienced by your brotherhood in the world.
— 1 Peter 5:8-9

Be careful where you trod. This world is packed with many traps
and snares which are presented just like the way the apple was
presented to our mother Eve in the Garden of Eden. If you're
not careful you will get allured by demons into a situation in
which you had no idea how terrible it would be and cannot find
a way of escape. Jesus taught us to be sober and be vigilant.
Pray for spiritual eyes to be opened to see the traps the devil
has set and is presenting as things beautiful and helpful, to the
natural eyes. Don't allow him to allure you.

God can help you. If you pray all the time and read, meditate
and study God's word you will be able to tell when the devil
is trying to trap you. Stay away from any movement that is
offering peace and contentment and all the fine things the body
and mind seeks for comfort through your own works away
from God. Movements like Transcendental Meditation, The
Unification Church, The Harry Krishna Movement, the Way
International, and the New Age Movement. These "movements"
are anti-Christ and are cults (obsessive worship of something
or someone other than the true and living God), and everyone
should stay away from such forms of worship as God warned
in His book the Holy Bible.

Prayer & Encouragement

Lord show us how to detect the devils scheme
and plots. Teach us to use wisdom and show us how
to overcome him. We pray in Jesus' name, Amen.

Do not worry about satan that old dragon,
Greater is He that is in us.

Put God First

But seek first the kingdom of God and His righteousness
and all these things shall be added to you.
– Matthew 6:33

The kingdom of God is righteousness, peace and joy in the Holy Ghost. - Romans 14:17. Therefore let us strive to keep a joyful spirit while doing the work of our Lord Jesus Christ in this earth. Let the Word of Christ dwell in us richly in all wisdom, teaching and admonishing each other in psalms and hymns and spiritual songs, singing with grace in our hearts to the Lord. - Colossians 3:16. The Lord knows all we have need of. He also knows those things we want or go after which will not benefit us. We go after them because of our lust which may cause us to sin if we're not careful. Our God is omniscient. He knows all things and therefore knows what is best for us. It is only wise to seek God's Kingdom and His righteousness and let Him seek out what's our best needs and provide for them as He knows best anyway. Seek Him today and leave everything else to Him. Put God first in your life and from all things you desire, God will bless you with those that will benefit you most.

Prayer & Encouragement

God help us not to be anxious for anything but in everything through prayer and supplication with thanksgiving make our request known. A sparrow doesn't fall to the ground without our Father's knowledge and He knows the number of hairs on your head. Don't worry or fret. You're of more value to God than a thousand sparrows.

Forgiveness

Then Peter asked Jesus,
"Lord how many times should my brother sin against me and
I forgive him? Up to seven times?" Jesus answered him,
"Not up to seven times but seventy times seven."
– Matthew 18:21-22

We must learn to forgive our brother each time he sins against us. Jesus teaches in this chapter of St. Matthew that if we do not forgive our brother when he sins against us then we will not be forgiven our sins either. This is God's law and He never breaks His law. In Matthew chapter 6 Jesus taught the disciples to pray on this fashion- Our Father in Heaven, hallowed be your name. Your kingdom come Your will be done on earth as it is in heaven. Give us this day our daily bread and forgive us our trespasses as we forgive those who trespass against us. Then He says if we forgive others their trespasses our heavenly Father will forgive our trespasses but if we do not forgive others neither will he forgive us. Matthew 6:9-15. The lesson is plain from this. Unless you want to stop or block your blessing, learn to forgive others. It's a choice.

Prayer & Encouragement

Lord teach us to forgive for as many times as is required. In Jesus name we pray. Teach us Lord to release our souls from self- imposed prisons. Help us to forgive ourselves and to also forgive others. Help us Lord to follow Your example of forgiveness. Amen!!! Forgiveness opens the door to so many wonderful things in our lives. We cannot afford not to forgive.

Bury It, Forget It, R.I.P.

Brethren, I do not count myself to have apprehended,
but one thing I do, forgetting those things which are behind
and reaching forward to those things which are ahead,
I press toward the goal for the prize of the
upward call of God in Christ Jesus.
– Philippians 3:13-14

Like Paul said under the inspiration of the Holy Spirit, forget the things which are behind that may keep you from getting ahead. There is no sense in dwelling on dead things which cannot and will not help us to get ahead in Christ Jesus. Read the Word of God and pray without ceasing daily. Then deeply meditate on God's Word so you may bury any past memories which the devil may try to use to haunt us or keep you in such a low state that you get blinded from seeing the glory set before you -the goal for the prize of the upward call of God in Christ Jesus. Strive to be who God created you to be, the original you, the one and only you in the world. Stay focused and work out your Salvation. Be diligent to make your calling and election sure. Be sober and vigilant for the enemy roams this earth as a roaring lion going to and fro upon it seeking whom he may devour. Don't fall prey to him. When he reminds you of your past, you remind him of his future.

Prayer & Encouragement

Father, may we always be aware that the major part of our Salvation process is that when we repent of our sins you forgive us and bury them in the "sea of forgetfulness" never to be remembered anymore. Help us to keep on moving

21

forward knowing we have a clean slate from you being justified by faith, regardless of what the lying devil or his elements in this earth says. Thank you Daddy, Amen.

Never allow the enemy to discourage you using your past. God our Father has buried them and no one is greater than your God. So move forward and fulfill your destiny knowing nothing from your past will be used to judge you on that great day. Jesus already paid it all.

A New Dimension in God

It's a new season. Some of God's children have come to realize that they're in this new season but don't know what exactly this means.

It's a new level, a new dimension in God.
This means new devils to deal with.

Also these devils hit harder, approach smarter and if one fails against them this can be devastating because these devils know that once you get to this level it means breakthrough to the most fulfilling moment in your walk with God. Therefore their intent is to destroy you, forever. It's a new dimension so don't be discouraged when you fail. Don't give up. Don't quit. Most of all don't listen to that devil. He knows just when to tempt you to give up or even try to annihilate you by getting you to do the things that will destroy you. Don't listen to them. Cry out to God even if it's from your heart (internally). He will come to your rescue. Then try your best to learn from each mistake. So when faced with this again you will know how to get through it successfully. And most important, never forget that Jesus is with you always (Matthew 28:20). He will not give up on you, ever!

Prayer and Encouragement

Lord grant us wisdom for each
new dimension we enter in You.
Don't give up. He who endures to the end
has a just reward to receive from our Lord.

Abba, Father

For you did not receive the spirit of bondage again to fear,
but you received the Spirit of adoption
by whom we cry out, Abba, Father."
– Romans 8:15

We first learned this Aramaic term when Jesus cried out in the Garden of Gethsemane, "Abba, Father, all things are possible for you. Take this cup away from Me ; nevertheless, not what I will, but what You will." (Mark 14:36). In both instances we see a deep, compassionate way in which the term is and should be used. God knows us intimately.

He knows us more closely than anyone else ever could and ever will. He knows us better than we know ourselves. He made every one of us and who knows anyone or anything better than its maker. He is our creator and our sustainer. He takes care of us better than our parents do and when parents are gone, He's the only one who does that role well in our eyes. That's when we become aware of His everlasting presence which was there all along before we became aware.

HE IS OUR FATHER. Our ABBA, FATHER. Hallowed be Your name our Abba, our Father. Your kingdom come and Your will be done here on earth as it is in heaven. Abba, Father, not our will but thine be done.

Prayer and Encouragement

Our Father, we bless Your Name for Who you were,
Who You are, and Who You forever will be. Abba, Father,
from everlasting to everlasting. You have no grandchildren.

All are Your children. Red, yellow, black and white,
we're all precious in Your sight. You made all things well.
Thank You Abba Father. In Jesus name we pray as joint-heirs
with Him. Amen!!! It feels so good to be a part of the family
of God. Aren't you glad that you're a part too?

Who's Your Daddy?

Doubtless You are our Father, though Abraham was ignorant
of us, and Israel does not acknowledge us. You, O Lord, are
our Father; our Redeemer from everlasting, is Your name.
– Isaiah 63:16

Many of us grew up not knowing our earthly (biological) father
until later in our lives. Some have never met their father. I didn't
meet my father until I was in high school and after that I saw
him rarely until he passed away in 1999 from complications
with diabetes and emphysema at the age of sixty-one. God
took the role of my father in the household and many things
I learned in my single parent home were through the grace of
God. The main thing I learned was to do my best to take care
of my children when I became a father, and I'm sure God would
say I've done well in that corner, thanks to Him. There are
many fathers today like myself who just want the best for their
children and will make the sacrifice to see that their children
turn out the best they can. We praise fathers at this time who
take the time to nurture and admonish their children in the way
God has commanded. To God be all the glory, the honor, and
the praise.

Prayer and Encouragement

Lord help us men to be the best fathers we can be,
not only to our children, but to all children. AMEN!!!

Fathers, only your best is good enough.
God Bless You!!!

26

He Knows You

The Lord has called you from the womb. From the bowels of your mother has He made mention of your name. He has made your mouth like a sharp sword; in the shadow of His hand has He hid you. And now says the Lord that formed you from the womb to be His servant, to bring you again to Him, though others be not gathered yet shall you be glorious in the eyes of the Lord and your God shall be your strength. Thus says the Lord, "In an acceptable time have I heard thee, and in a day of salvation have I helped thee, and I will preserve thee, and give thee for a covenant of the people, to establish thee; that you may say to the prisoners, go forth; to them that are in darkness, show yourselves." They shall not hunger nor thirst; neither shall the heat nor sun smite them, even by the springs of water shall He guide them. And God will make all His mountains a way, and His highways shall be exalted. Sing, O heavens, and be joyful, O earth, break forth into singing O mountains, for the Lord has comforted His people, and will have mercy upon His afflicted. But Zion said, the Lord has forsaken me, and my Lord has forsaken me. Can a woman forget her sucking child that she should not have compassion on the son of her womb? Yes, they may forget, yet I will not forget you. Behold I have graven you upon the palm of my hands; thy walls are continually before me. Thank you for the assurance that You know me.

Prayer and Encouragement

Thank You Lord that I can always run to You for advice.
You know me better than I know myself.
God knows everything, and I mean everything about you.

Know Whose You Are

I have called you by your name, you are mine.
– Isaiah 43:1

We all need to know who we are in the Lord and whose we are. Our God calls us by our names, chooses us and makes us His. We are children of our God. We are children of our King. We are children of our Father in heaven. We are His. Before He formed us in the womb He knew us. And when we came forth from our mothers He sanctified and ordained us for the work He plans for us to do. There's no reason for anyone to get uptight when they see you being blessed. They have their hour too according to our Father's plan. Just humbly tell whoever is saying negatives about you, especially throwing your past at you, "GET OVER IT!!!" We all have our time and our season. Tell someone to be happy for you as that will speed up their season of blessings to them.

Prayer & Encouragement

Father we pray that everyone will be happy for each other when the blessings overtake each one of us. In Jesus' name we pray. AMEN.

We each have a time for God's blessing plan. Let us be happy for others while awaiting ours.

He Promised To Be With Us

The LORD is my shepherd; I shall not want.
– Psalm.23:1

God promised to be with us through "thick and thin" until the end of the age. He will never leave us nor forsake us. Jesus will be with us everywhere we go and in everything we go through. God will take care of us while we're here and even in eternity. Is there anyone in God's Kingdom who has a need today? He said we shall not want and He will supply our needs. His word says in Philippians 4:19, "My God shall supply all your needs according to His riches in glory by Christ Jesus." His word also says in Ps 37:25, " I have been young and now I am old; yet have I not seen the righteous forsaken nor his seed begging bread." Jesus says He is the good shepherd. All else who look after the sheep are hirelings who flees when they see the wolf coming and scattering the sheep but He lays down His life for the sheep. (John 10:11-15). He is committed to our welfare.

Prayer and Encouragement

Father we thank you for being there for us and sending your Son to lay down His life for us. Help us keep in mind that your Son, our Savior, Jesus Christ, the good shepherd, is always with us taking care of our every need. In His name we do pray, Amen! Whatever you're going through, Jesus is with you, seeing to your every need.

He Restores

The Lord answered (David), "Pursue, for you shall surely
overtake them and without fail recover all."
– 1 Samuel 30:8b (AMP).

When God is with you and pleased with your worship whatever
is taken from you by the enemy, the Lord will help you overtake
that enemy and recover everything. David and his men's family
and all their possessions were taken by the Amalekites who
plundered and burned their homes in Ziklag. When they all
returned home and saw what happened, all the men spoke of
stoning David saying it was his fault that this had taken place.
David found himself a "safe" place and encouraged himself
in the Lord. Then he asked the Lord if he should pursue the
Amalekites and God told him to pursue for he will overtake
them and recover everything. If you ever find yourself in a
situation where it seems there is no way out and you're the one
responsible for this situation, don't let discouragement cause
you to give up. Look to the Lord and pray for His leading and
direction because He will surely bring you out and will make
sure you have all you need every step of the way. He will see
to it that you recover all.

Prayer & Encouragement

Help us Father never to give up but always
seek your guidance and leadership. Amen.
When you are down and out, God will surely
bring you out. Never give up. Don't quit!

Lord You Know Me

O Lord You have searched me and have known me.
– Psalm139:1

Lord You know me better than I know myself. You knew me before You formed me in my mother's womb. You sanctified me and ordained me upon arrival in this earth. You ordained me a prophet unto nations. You knew every mistake I would make during my lifetime. You knew my past before it became my past and You know my future. Nothing is hidden from your eyes. Lord You have been our dwelling place throughout all generations. Before the mountains were brought forth or ever you had formed the earth and the world, even from everlasting to everlasting thou art God. You are an awesome God. What a mighty God we serve. The heavens declare Your glory O God and the firmament, Your handiwork. Lord wherever I go or wherever I find myself You are already there. You were there waiting for me. How cool is that?

Prayer & Encouragement

Lord nothing is hidden from You. Why should we not trust You to take care of us as You carry out Your plan for each one of us here on Your earth individually and collectively. We thank you for revelation knowledge. In Jesus' name, Amen. Trust God. He made us for His purpose anyway

What is For You Is for You

Son you are always with me and all that is mine is yours
– Luke 15:31

There is no need for anyone to be jealous of a brother or a sister in the kingdom. No one can take what is yours and you cannot have what is someone else's. There can only be one you. No carbon copy exist. You're the original. All that the Father has for you is for you and you alone. Now that's something to shout about. So the next time you feel jealousy trying to show its ugly head, you let jealousy know. You're quite satisfied with who you are and where you are. No need to be jealous. No one can have what's yours.

Prayer & Encouragement

God help us to keep in mind that all that you have for each one of us is for that person and no one else therefore, there's no need to be jealous of anyone else. Amen.

Praise God for your uniqueness and
continue in the work of the Lord.

A Good Soldier of Jesus Christ

You therefore must endure hardship
as a good soldier of Jesus Christ.
– 2 Timothy 2:3

A soldier is trained to face anything that he encounters and to do his best to emerge victorious. The tasks faced by soldiers most times are life threatening but the soldier must never retreat or surrender. The soldier is also trained to obey all orders of his superior officers without hesitation or question. In God's Kingdom all Christians are seen as soldiers who function in much the same way as soldiers in the world. We however are in spiritual warfare and so our weapons are not carnal (physical) but spiritual (prayer, praise, the Word of God etc.) and whereas the soldier in the world knows not the outcome of each battle he fights we know we've already won the ultimate battle. Therefore we're encouraged by Paul to endure hardship as a good soldier as we know there's always something good to gain from our "hard" experiences.

Prayer and Encouragement

Lord help us to keep in mind that as we endure hardship we've already won this war and are just learning from our experiences to help us in future ones. Therefore we should count it all joy when we fall into trials knowing that the testing of our faith works patience. In Jesus precious name we pray. Amen! Endure whatever you come up against using the spiritual weapons God has provided. When you get to the end there are great rewards to obtain.

Be an Eagle

But they that wait upon the Lord shall renew their strength.
They shall mount up with wings as eagles, they shall run and
not be weary, they shall walk and not faint.
– Isaiah 40:31

Samuel when handing over the prophetic mantle to Nathan told him, "Stay close to David and give him the counsel he needs because God doesn't make it easy for a king to rule His people." I would add that no preparation for God's work is "easy." God leads His children beside still waters, somewhere in the valley below. Then He pulls each one aside to be tested and tried and in the valley He restores their souls. When it's preparation time for a Godly task, one will find himself in an isolated state. No one can go with you through your preparation. Everyone, it will seem, has abandoned you. Why? They cannot go through with you. This was not for them and if anyone tries to go with you when they shouldn't, the process may kill them.

So as you're going through, it will seem tough
but watch yourself soar in the midst of it.
You're an eagle so mount up on your wings.

Eagles soar to great heights and get a bird's eye view of God's work in progress. At such great heights no one else soars, because they don't have the ability to see from such heights as the eagle. While you're going through alone, build up your patience because it doesn't matter how long this preparation takes your strength will be renewed in it. You shall grow stronger and stronger.

You will be better and better. God will not give up on you. Have you not known? Have you not heard? The everlasting God, the

34

Lord, The creator of the ends of the earth, neither faints nor is weary. His understanding is unsearchable, He gives power to the weak, and to those who have no might He increases strength. Even the youths shall faint and be weary, and the young men shall utterly fall. But they that wait upon the Lord shall renew their strength; they shall mount up with wings like eagles, they shall run and not be weary, they shall walk and not faint. - Isaiah 40:28-31

Prayer & Encouragement

Lord teach us to wait on you during our preparation and never give up. When the time comes Lord help us to soar like eagles. Help us to have keen vision. Help us to renew our strength. Help us Lord to find our identity and recognize who we are in You. O Lord You are the source of our strength. Thank You Jesus!!!! Hallelujah!!!! Amen.

Whatever God takes you through, it is because He loves you and cares about you very much and the process is beneficial to you. Stay the course with Him. Remember, You are stronger than you think you are.

Testimony of an Overcomer

And we overcame (the accuser of the brethren) by the
blood of the Lamb and by the word of our testimony.
– Revelation 12:11

God says that nothing shall separate us from His love. Not tribulation nor distress, nor persecution nor famine, nor nakedness nor peril nor sword. In all these things we are more than conquerors, we are victorious. We are overcomers. For neither death nor life, nor angels nor principalities nor powers, nor things present nor things to come, nor height nor depth, nor any other created thing, shall be able to separate us from the love of God which is in Christ Jesus our Lord (Rom. 8:35-39). The accuser has been standing to accuse us for a long time and each time he does he is rebuked and rebuffed (Zechariah 3:1,2; Revelation:10).

The Lord stands triumphantly as our advocate because His finish work on the cross has paid for our sins, past, present and future. We have overcome the world and its laws of sin and shame and the prince of it all by the blood of the Lamb and by the word of our testimony.

Whatever you find yourself going through at this time do not let yourself be deceived. Pray and praise God through it. You will come out victorious. You will overcome. Why? Because we are overcomers.

Prayer & Encouragement

Lord let us never lose sight that we are overcomers
when faced with any challenge. Amen.

You have no need to doubt or fear
when you are up against the enemy.
Be of good cheer.
Greater is He who is in you than he who is in the world.
Because He's in us, we are overcomers.

We Are More than Conquerors

"No weapon formed against you shall prosper, and every
tongue that rises against you in judgment, you shall condemn.
This is the heritage of the servants of the LORD, and
their righteousness is from me," says the LORD.
– Isaiah 54:17

So many of our brothers and sisters are suffering in different countries in the world where the government has no respect or regard for God or His children. One most notable country where Christians are grossly oppressed is North Korea. The latest news out of this country is that young women are being smuggled into China by other people of the same nationality who sell these young ladies for exorbitant sums of money after which these ladies are forced to be sex slaves. If they refuse they run the risk of being turned over to the security force in North Korea where they'll be imprisoned for attempting to defect to China. Today many of these women are being rescued from these slavery conditions and are being trained to become evangelists and sent back to North Korea to help others there to spread the gospel and win souls to Christ. What the enemy meant for evil God is turning into good. No weapon formed against us shall prosper.

Prayer and Encouragement

Lord thank you for helping to overcome each evil plan of the enemy. Help us to always trust You and lean and depend on You. Amen. Whatever the situation you're going through, don't give up. It's never over until God says it's over and He'll never leave you nor forsake you

You're An Overcomer

He that overcometh shall inherit all things;
and I will be his God, and he shall be my son.
– Revelation 21:7

When you find yourself in situations which you have no control, cry out, "Abba, Father, with You all things are possible. Deliver me through this or out of it immediately please. Not my will but thine be done!" When you find yourself in situations which you have no control, cry out, "Abba, Father, with You all things are possible. Deliver me through this or out of it immediately please. Not my will but thine be done!" Remember that no weapon formed against you shall prosper. The Holy Spirit comes to our aid and bears us up in our weakness; for we do not know what prayer to offer nor how to offer it worthily as we ought, but the Spirit Himself goes to meet our supplication and pleads in our behalf with unspeakable yearnings and groaning too deep for utterance. Romans.8:26. We need to start pulling down some strongholds in the name of Jesus and plea the blood of Jesus over our household and extended families. The enemy is very busy as he's aware his time is running out. Alkanai undaaa!!!!

Prayer and Encouragement

Thank you Father, for making us overcomers. Lord help us
to know Your Word and to stand bold and confidently
on Your Word. Help us to believe Your promises.
Help us to see ourselves as You see us.
Victorious. More Than a Conqueror. Blessed.
You're an overcomer. Walk in your authority.

Only Trust Him

But He knows the way that I take,
when He has tested me, I shall come forth as gold.
– Job 23:10

Whatever we experience in life as Christians, our God knows. Everyone in this world is either going through something, coming out of something or about to go through something. Wherever you are, be confident of this one thing, God knows the way you take and when He has tested you, you shall come forth as pure gold. No impurities left behind after going through the fire. God knows every path everyone takes and He knows how everything for everyone will turn out. There are three types of suffering in this world. There is the suffering due to this world being a sinful and adulterous one. Second there is the suffering we bring onto ourselves through our own actions and third, we may be brought through a painful experience to strengthen and prepare us for an assignment from the Lord (like Job). Either way God will help His children to go through and come forth successful. Like Job we all can be successful and receive our great rewards from God both here on earth and in eternity. Only trust God to bring you through and bring you out, He who began a good work in you will complete it against the day of Jesus Christ.

Prayer & Encouragement

Father wherever we are in life, help us to trust you as you
bring us to perfection. Help us to know Lord that
NO MATTER what life brings our way we can trust
You to bring us through it!!! Amen. Only trust God.

Don't Worry, Be Happy

For we know that all things work together for good to those who
love God, to those who are the called according to His purpose.
– Romans 8:28

Whatever is happening in your life today that may seem
unbearable, understand that the enemy might mean it for evil,
but God will make it good. All things work together for the
good of those who love the Lord. You may go through the fire
or you may go through the flood, you may have been broken
in pieces or seen lightening flash from above. Know this for
sure, He will never put more on you than you can bear. Now we
know God doesn't tempt anyone nor is He tempted by anyone
and He doesn't bring trials, persecutions and/or tribulations
on us. He allows these things, and then take us through and
out victoriously when we let Him. This is how scripture puts
it. No temptation has overtaken you but such as is common to
man; but God is faithful, who will not allow you to be tempted
beyond what you are able, but will with the temptation also
make a way of escape. - 1 Corinthians 10:13. Then if, we falter
during a trial He has a plan in place for that too. If we confess
that sin or those sins to God, He is faithful and just to forgive
us of these sins and to cleanse us from all unrighteousness. So
you see, all things work together for the good to those who love
the Lord, to those who are the called according to His purpose.

Prayer & Encouragement

Lord help us to not worry and be happy because You have
all the bases covered in our fragile lives. Amen. He's got the
whole world in His hands and if you know He's keeping you,
what are you going to worry about.

The Joy of the Lord Is Your Strength

Do not sorrow, for the joy of the Lord is your strength.
– Nehemiah 8:10

Sometimes you may be wondering what am I doing here? Why am I here? Where am I going? What's going to happen to me? Who do I trust? Where can I go for answers to my so many questions about life? Who am I? What is life about? And so on, and so on, and so on. Questions like these sometimes lead to frustration and sometimes even worse, suicide. If you're thinking about anything like that as the answer to your questions and sorrows, I want you to know there is a better way.

There is someone who has all the answers you are seeking and even more comfort and pleasure than you could ever imagine. I want you to know that the moment you make Him your friend you will find the love you have been seeking, which no one else would give you. You will find a peace that is above anyone's understanding. You will find a strength you never knew you had. For His joy at you accepting Him will become your strength.

He gives you that joy which is unspeakable (unexplainable). You will find that "things" may have happened to you that bothered you before but now it is nothing to you, because of a joy you have, which no one else could give you and no one else can take away from you. Try Him today. His name is Jesus. He'll be anything you want Him to be. His joy is your strength. He'll never leave you once you invite Him into your life. Oh, once you try Him and then realize what you have been missing in your life to make you complete is in Him, you're going to wish you had accepted Him long before now. I know, I've been there.

Prayer & Encouragement

Lord we pray for everyone who reads this devotional and is led to accept Jesus Christ, the answer to every question, the solution to every problem, in their hearts, in Jesus' name, Amen. Try Jesus. You'll realize that His joy is your strength.

You're Holy God

Father we're coming before Your throne of grace this morning in the mighty name of Jesus. We give You the glory this morning Lord. Your name is wonderful. Your name is marvelous, Jesus Christ our Lord. We give you the honor, the glory and the praise. Our Father we exalt Your holy and righteous name on today. Majesty, we worship and adore You today!!! We're thankful to You for laying us down last night, watching over us as we slumbered through the night and touching us with Your finger of divine love and helping us to rise on this brand new day which we've never seen before and will never see again. The perfect day. The day which You made for us because You know the best day for us each morning. Thank You for making sure we rose in our right minds. Thank You just for the opportunity to see this day. It's a wonderful privilege and we do not take it for granted our Father. Father forgive us our trespasses; those we're aware of and those we're not aware of. The sins of commission and those of omission. Blot out our transgression from before Your face our Father and wash us and cleanse us in the blood of Jesus Christ. Thank You Father. Now Father we ask You to reveal Your agenda, Your plans for us today Lord. Then grant us all we stand in need of to fulfill Your plans for today our God. Help us to do our part individually and collectively wherever needed to complete this big picture which we can only see our part of. Help us to take no thought for tomorrow but focus on today as sufficient unto this day is all the challenges we have to face in it our God. Help us to live one day at a time Father. In other words our Father help us to make this day the best day of our lives ever. Thank You for Your word which takes us along safely and securely in our life's journey. Thank You for prayer which takes us in Your presence and away from the enemy Satan. Thank you for praise our God which lifts us out of discouraging emotions like depression Lord. Thank You for

44

all the spiritual weapons of our warfare and the whole armor You have given to us. The breastplate of righteousness, the helmet of Salvation, the belt of truth, the shoes of the Gospel of Jesus Christ, the shield of faith, the sword of the Spirit which is the Word of God and prayers of thanksgiving, intercession and supplication etc. We thank You that while nothing has been mentioned in Your armor to protect our backs You see that we don't need anything as surely Goodness and Mercy follows us all the days of our lives providing all the protection we need from behind. THANK YOU LORD!!! In the name of the Father, the Son and the Holy Ghost we pray today and close in Jesus' name. Amen!!!!!

Prayer and Encouragement

Lord, teach us how to pray.
In Matthew chapter. 6, Jesus gives us a model prayer.

- Praise of our Father - Recognition of God's will in our lives.
- Petitions for our needs, for forgiveness, and deliverance
- Recognition of God's eternal might.

Who is He?

For God so love the world that He gave His only begotten Son that whosoever believeth in Him should not perish but have everlasting life.
– John 3:16

Many in the world have still not heard about our Jesus. Others are still wondering if all the things they've heard about Him are true. Still there are some not sure if He ever existed or can He still be alive, as many claim Him to be. Who is He? Many are asking and I'm glad they are, for it affords me an opportunity to glorify the true and living God in answering you.

He, first and foremost is God's only begotten Son. He is second in the Godhead (Father, Son, and Holy Ghost), In Him we live and move and have our being. By Him all things consists. He is the bread of life (John 6:35, 41, 48, 51); the light of the world (John 8:12; 9:5); the door for His sheep (10:7,9); the good shepherd (John 10:11,14) the resurrection and the life (John 11:25); the way the truth and the life (John 14: 6); and the true vine (John 15:1).

You will notice in the gospel of John that each of these statements when spoken by Jesus begins with I AM recalling God's revelation to Moses (Exod. 3:14). Jesus signifies here that He is God and will be whatever anyone wants Him to be in their situation or need.

Jesus is the doctor in a sickroom, the lawyer in a courtroom, the teacher in a classroom, preacher, way maker, a bridge over troubled water, rock in a weary land, a battle-axe, our banner, healer, leader, servant, anything you want Him to be, He will be. His Name is Jesus Our Savior and Lord, Our Wonderful Counselor, Mighty God, Everlasting Father, and Prince of Peace.

46

Prayer and Encouragement

Lord, just when we think we know everything there is to
know about you there come new revelations.
Help us to know you. Amen.

Establish a relationship with Jesus.
You will be able to tell others
He is alive and real deep down in your soul.

God's Gifts

The Lord says, "Fear not, I am your shield, your abundant compensation, and your reward shall be exceedingly great."

God says,
"All that you're able to 'see'
I will give to you and to
Your posterity forever."

Praise the Lord for His "indescribable" gifts,
His good and perfect gifts from above.

God wants someone to be encouraged this morning. He says, "In blessing I will bless you and in multiplying I will multiply your descendants like the stars of the heavens and like the sand on the seashore. And your seed (heir) will possess the gate of his enemies."

Prayer and Encouragement
Lord thank you for your promises.
God keeps all His promises.

The God Who Comforts

May the God of all grace, who called us to His eternal glory through
Christ Jesus, perfect, establish, strengthen and settle you.
– 1 Peter 5:10

This text tells us that suffering is meant to perfect, establish,
strengthen, and settle us (*cf. Heb. 12:5,6*) The greek used here
offers insight on what God wants to accomplish through this
process. *Katartizo* (perfect) means to complete what is lacking;
sterizo (establish) points us toward turning resolutely in a certain
direction; *sthenoo (s*trengthen) means to confirm in spiritual
knowledge and power; and *themelioo* (settle) refers to the laying
of a foundation. Be encouraged today!!! Suffering or trial, in
whatever area of life you're experiencing it, will be used to
further God's purpose in you. He is making you complete.
Setting you on His path, filling you with spiritual strength, and
laying the foundation of your future. He promised never to leave
you nor forsake you and He knows every temptation we face and
the ordeal we go through with each one, seeing He was tempted
in every way as we are right now. He is right there with you
going through with you while encouraging you all the way never
to give up. It may seem long sometimes but remember His Word
which says, "Weeping may endure for a night but joy cometh in
the morning. I know the night may seem long sometimes and
morning may seem like it's never coming, but His Word never
goes out and comes back to Him void but accomplishes what it
is sent forth to. Also He says He hastens to perform His Word.
Therefore what may seem to take days, weeks, or months may
happen in a day when He gets ready to perform it. Take comfort
in His Word. Hold on my brother. Hold on my sister. Don't give
up. Don't quit. Quitters never win and winners never quit.

Prayer and Encouragement

Lord help us never to throw in the towel regardless of how it looks.
Don't you ever, ever, give up on God. He will never give up on you!

God Is Eternal

I am He who lives, and was dead,
and behold I am alive forevermore. Amen.
And I have the keys of Hades and of death.
– Revelation 1:18

While in prayer about a matter that troubles me terribly regarding the lifestyle of many of my fellow countrymen and women and the fact that those in authority seem to support this lifestyle wholeheartedly even though most in leadership still practice the proper lifestyle (in regards to this issue), my God spoke to me in the midst of my complaining. He said to me, "Let me take you back to your childhood in the country you were born." Then He showed me the atrocities which were taking place in my country during my childhood. Some I witnessed firsthand others through the different media.

I was a third generation child at the time. The first generation to face these "hardcore violence" were wounding and sometimes killing each other by cutting with knives, broken pieces of bottles and ice-pricks among other sharp objects, and stoning each other to death. The second generation started out shooting each other with small handguns, then went on to use high power assault weapons and machine guns. By the time the third generation grew up (which I mentioned before that I belonged to), there were a few who were "brainwashed" into believing this was the norm. However the majority of us were tired of this disrespect for the value of human lives and useless killing. We took a stand and brought violence to its lowest in thirty years. Of course there is the usual flare-ups but they are quickly extinguished by our generation.

Then the Lord said to me. Have you noticed that most times when the wicked seem to be blossoming among the rest of the world's population, they don't last forever? Then you need not worry regardless of how things look. Evil may go on for a long time in human eyes but it is fleeting in mine. I am here forever and these times shall pass. A new generation will rise up that includes political leaders who will no longer tolerate this evil that is being embraced by the present generation. As the saying goes: Time is the healer of all wounds (Proverbially speaking). So when the enemy seem to be spreading his evil wicked wings like a green bay tree. Don't worry. Don't fret. After a while they are no longer around. Good always outlive and override evil. Lies will parade itself as truth and reach halfway around the world before truth even has a chance to lace up its bootstraps. But eventually truth will appear and lie will then be extinguished. Hear the conclusion of the whole matter, fear God and keep His commandments, for this is all that is required of man. God will bring everything into judgment, including every secret thing, whether good or evil (Eccl. 12:13-14).

Prayer and Encouragement

Lord thank you for always having the answer.
Thank You Lord. You are the answer.
Whatever the problem, take it to the Lord in prayer.
He's been here forever and will be here forever.
He has all the answers because He knows the
end from the beginning. He is omniscient.

God's Word Is Sure

Regardless of what you're facing right now God's word is true and will be fulfilled. He says, "Before I formed thee in the belly I knew thee, and before thou came forth out of the womb I sanctified thee, and I ordained thee a prophet unto the nations." Jeremiah 1:5. It doesn't matter what your life is like right now. Even if you feel like God could not accept you after all you've been through or all that you've done. Believe me when you were going through or doing all that you were doing God was not for one moment surprised or shock. God knew everything that would happen in your entire life before you were even born. His Word says, "And in Your book they all were written, the days fashioned for me, when as yet there were none of them." Psalm 139:16b. And because He knows your past, and present he already planned for your future to be much, much better when you accept Him as your Savior and Lord. You don't know how He will do it and you most certainly don't want to know or else you may change your mind. But this one thing you can be sure of, He will make you have a much better life. John 10:10

Prayer and Encouragement

Lord I pray for my brother and my sister right now as they try to make the right decision to serve you.

My brother, my sister, there is no regret when anyone accepts Jesus as his/her personal Savior and Lord.

God's Blessings

All these blessings shall come on you, and overtake you,
if you hearken to the voice of the Lord.
– Deuteronomy 28:2

Have you ever meditated on this scripture?
1 Timothy 6:17 says,
"He gives us richly all things to enjoy."

God is a loving father.
He gets pleasure from blessing His children.
He can afford to.

Once you believe and hearken to His voice,
it won't be long before His blessings overtake you.

Prayer and Encouragement

Thank You for Your plans for us Lord.
His plans are what's best for us.
Accept them today.

That's Why I Love Him

"For God so love the world that he gave His only begotten
Son that whosoever believes in Him shall
not perish but have eternal life."
– John 3:16

He does so much for me. If He hasn't done anything more for me, He has done so much already it's more than enough. Why does He do all this? Because He loves me so much. A songwriter says, O how He loves us so. O how He loves us.

Even if He didn't do anything more for me I would still love Him because of who He is. He is love. He loves us. Oh how He loves us. We can never fathom the depth, height, width, length or any other measurement of His love for us.

THANK YOU GOD
FOR LOVING US SO MUCH.

His Word says, "For God so love the world that he gave His only begotten Son that whosoever believes in Him shall not perish but have eternal life." John 3:16. All that and much more is why I love Him.

Prayer and Encouragement

God, thank You for loving us so much.
If you do not know Him and
His love for us, try Him today.
You will never live to regret it.

Great Is Your Faithfulness

Great is Your faithfulness.
– Lamentations 3:23

Great is thy faithfulness! Great is thy faithfulness! Morning by morning new mercies I see; All I have needed Thy hand hath provided; Great is thy faithfulness, Lord, unto me!

A beautiful hymn that shows God's great faithfulness to us. The verse preceding the text above says, "Through the Lord's mercies we're not consumed, because His compassions fail not. They are new every morning..." Let us bless the Lord at all times and let His praises be in your mouth from the rising of the sun until the going down of the same, every day. Even today!!!

Prayer & Encouragement

Lord thank You for Your great faithfulness to us. Thank You, thank You, thank You, thank You. Thank You for waking us up each morning and helping us to see a brand new day. Thank You Lord for giving us, hopes, dreams and vision to live life full of purpose. No goodness of our own. Thank You Lord I know I can always count on You to be faithful in my life.

Praise God at all times for His faithfulness.

He Brings Life

The thief comes only to steal, kill and destroy. I (Jesus)
have come that you might have life in abundance.
– John 10:10

Jesus said He is the bread of life, the fountain of living water, the door for the sheep, the good shepherd, the light of the world, the way, the truth and the life, and the resurrection and life. Whoever believes in Him though he were dead he shall live again, and whosoever lives and believes in Him shall never die. Jesus came to seek and to save those who are lost and he came that all may have life and have it more abundantly. The thief hates all mankind who are created by God but God loves us tremendously. He cares about our welfare and our joy. It is His good pleasure to give us of the kingdom. He wants to do more for us than we could ever ask or imagine but we must first come to Him and ask, seek and knock so we will receive, find and have doors open to us. Nothing can stop God from doing His good pleasure for us but we need to accept what He has for us as He will not force His will unto us. Search the scriptures for in them you will find God's perfect will for your lives which is the truth and when you do find this truth it will set you free.

Prayer and Encouragement

Lord teach us where we lack knowledge of Your will and Your way. Amen. Ask and you shall receive, seek and you will find, knock and the door will be opened to you. But first, know what to ask for according to God's will and ask in Jesus' name. Know that what you're seeking is according to His will. And when a door is closed and doesn't open move to the next door.
Be sure you're moving in His perfect will.

He Calls Me Friend

I'd rather walk in the dark with God than go alone in the light;
I'd rather walk by faith with Him than go alone by sight.

Where God Guides He Provides

Remember the old saying, to make friends one has to be friendly, it is still true and effective today. To be a good friend, we must love others, respect others, understand people, and care for people. Have a heart to help when there is the need for it. Jesus said, no longer do I call you servants, but I have called you friends. That is why we can cast all our cares on Him. In other words, it's not just what we can get out of a friendship but what we may give into it that will be of benefit to the friends involved. That is so wonderful, Jesus calls me His friend. That is what I call friendship with benefit. I am a friend of God and so are you!!! Everyone, if you're feeling what I'm feeling as you read this, if you feel God's presence so close that you're being overshadowed right now then please join me in this brief prayer...

Prayer and Encouragement

Thank You God for making me your friend. Amen!!!
Make Jesus your friend today.

He Will Never Forsake His Own

"I will never leave you nor forsake you."
– Hebrews 13:5

An earthquake and tsunami just hit the island of Japan a few hours ago and other countries are now waiting to see if they will be hit by a tsunami as well. Many people may be fearful. Others may be worried while some may be confused. The question in minds right now may be, "Where is God whenever events of this nature is taking place?" One possible answer may be that He is right here with us.

He promised he will never leave us nor forsake us. He sees everything while they are happening and he hasn't lost control. These things happen because of the world we are living in and are signs of the time (see Mathew chapter 24 or Luke chapter 21). We as Christ's followers need to take note of the happenings around us, know that God is in full control and look up for our redemption draws nigh.

Prayer & Encouragement

Father please give us wisdom and strength to enlighten and assist others in times of disasters and crises. In Jesus' name we pray. Amen. Pray for wisdom and strength among everything else you need in the time of disaster and/or crises.

He Makes All Things New

Then He who sat on the throne said,
"Behold I make all things new."
– Revelation 21:5

God does keep His promises. In the book of Jeremiah He promised to give us a new heart (Jer. 31:31-34) and He most certainly fulfilled that promise over four hundred and fifty years later. Paul confirmed this in 2 Cor. 5:17 when he stated, "Therefore, if anyone is in Christ, he is a new creation, old things have passed away; behold all things have become new."

Behold He makes all things new.

In Isaiah 43:19 God says Behold He will do a new thing. Now it shall spring forth; shall we not know it? He fulfilled the law at Calvary and reassured us when He stated, "It is finished." That was the beginning of Grace Dispensation. Behold, the New Testament, the New Covenant ratified in the Blood of Jesus Christ, The new beginning was established. Behold God has done a new thing. He has made all things new.

Prayer & Encouragement

Lord we want to continue to do our part in bringing others to you so they may become new creations in you as you continue to make all things new in the earth realm. Thank you for your plan and purpose for all of us, your children. Amen. Don't miss out on God's indescribable gift to you. Behold He makes all things new.

His Promises Are Sure

When Rachel's second son was born, she named him Ben-
Oni, "son of my sorrow," before she died. Jacob renamed
the baby Benjamin, or" son of my right hand."
– Genesis 35:18

The family (Jacob's family) had just got to Ephratha, the ancient
name for Bethlehem. Similarly, from Mary's perspective,
Jesus who would also be born in Bethlehem, would be the
"son of (her) sorrow" (Luke 2:35, John 19:25), but to God He
is the "son of my right hand" (Hebrews 1:3). From the "man of
sorrows" (Isaiah 53:3), Jesus was exalted to the "Lord of glory"
(1 Corinthians 2:8). Despite facing obstacles and griefs in our
daily lives, God never fails to fulfill His gracious promises
to us. But that fulfillment is often contingent upon our own
willingness to trust and obey. He tells us in the gospel of John
that if we abide in Him and His word abides in us we can ask
of the Father what we will in His name and He will grant it to
us. Also in Psalms 37:4 we're told that if we delight ourselves
in Him, He will give us the desires of our hearts. Isn't the love
of Jesus something wonderful Praise His holy name.

Prayer and Encouragement

Lord help us to trust You to fulfill your promises in us.
Trust and obey Jesus and watch wonders performed
in your life according to his promises and His will.
You may be a son of sorrows in other people's eyes but God
will make you a son of His right hand if you'll allow Him!!!

He is the God of Divine Wisdom

God chooses the weak and small to confound the strong.
– 1 Corinthians. 1:27

God wishes to let everyone in this earth know that He is the one doing the work being done through His servants. Therefore when we see someone we think is a reject or insignificant person in society doing something we know within ourselves this person should not know how to do.

Know of a certainty, it is God doing
what's being done through the person.

Sometimes the action may even be beyond our natural ability and that's when we should realize God is not only doing it, but He is telling us something. In addition to the message, He is also letting us know that by using someone in society's judgment as insignificant, He is showing that He does exist and since this person could never do this act on his/her own it is Him (God) doing it.

The next time God tells you who are His, to do something and it seems foolish to you, don't question it. This could be your moment to be used by God to confound the wise and strong.

Prayer & Encouragement

Father help us to ALWAYS Trust and obey you.
He loves us so much, He's willing to show us off whenever
He pleases. Do not doubt when He tells you to do something.
Just do it with no question or hesitation.

His Blessings Are New Each Day

Through the Lord's mercies we are not consumed, because
His compassions fail not. They are new every morning;
great is Your faithfulness.
– Lamentations 3:22-23.

When our youngest son was three years old and in pre-k there was one thing for sure his mother and I have realized from his learning in school and that is, he is sharp when it comes to detecting moods and attitudes. Almost every day he asked his mother and I if we're happy, sad or mad. Even when we least think about it because we're so engaged in some activity or chore. I mention this because we sometimes may be in either one of these moods and may be totally unaware of it when it does matter to others around us. God's blessings are sure each day regardless of the mood we may find ourselves in.

Through His mercies we are not consumed. Our righteousness are as filthy rags before Him. There is none righteous, no not one. Thank God our Father for Jesus our Savior and Lord who through taking our sins unto Himself has made us righteous; that is Jesus' righteousness is now what God our Father sees in us. Our Father is faithful to us with all His promises, some conditional, however He keeps them all. He is faithful to bless us each and every day and it is up to us to receive these blessings. Don't let any pass you by and do not block any either. Receive from the Lord today. It's His good pleasure to give us of His kingdom.

Prayer & Encouragement

Lord help us to receive Your blessings every day from the rising of the sun until the going down of the same as we send the praises up to you simultaneously. We praise you for every blessing and most of all for who You are. Amen. Try your best not to miss out on any of God's blessings that is meant for you each day.

He's Always On Time

Now Jesus loved Martha and her sister and Lazarus.
So when He heard that he was sick, He stayed
two more days in the place where He was.
– John 11:5-6

Our God may not move or work on our schedule and sometimes situation may seem dire to us. Other times it may seem like, if our God does not come through for us right then and there, then all hope is gone. Our God shows up whenever He is ready. Whenever He knows the time is right. He is not governed or hindered by time. Even if it was an illness that resulted in death and the person has been buried. Even then God is still able to command that person to rise from his dead state. After all, He is the resurrection and the life! (John 11:25) Someone may be going through a fiery trial and is wondering when God come through for them.

Don't you worry, and don't you fret. Just keep on praying and believing. He will come through for you. He may not come when you want Him but He's always on time. The number one most wanted terrorist in the world was just killed in a firefight in Pakistan on Sunday May 1, 2011. This man is responsible for the death of nearly three thousand Americans on September 11, 2001.

Many may still be asking where God was on that dreadful day. God was right there before the first plane hit and He was there as each person died in Him. He received each one into heaven with him and although many grieve for love ones to this day, these love ones are in a better place and would never return to a world like this if they had the choice. Not to take anything from any family member or friend left behind here. Your love one still cares. Understand that they are now praying that you too will someday soon, come to where they are and enjoy what they are enjoying, once God's purpose is fulfilled in your life.

Prayer & Encouragement

Lord teach us faith, hope and patience to trust you to come to our aid on time, when we think you're not there when we expect you to. Amen.

Hold on just a little while longer. He's always on time.

He Is Real

He was in the world, and the world was made
through Him, and the world did not know Him.
– John 1:10

Although God shows His existence in so many different ways, there are many who still say they do not believe in Him. Some go as far as to say they don't believe that a God exist or is real especially seeing that they have never seen Him. I say to all the unbelievers, because you can't see electricity, is it real? Stick your hand in a socket every now and again and you'll be reminded that even though you can't see it, electricity is real. Another example is having a tooth-ache. Even though you can't see or touch the pain you know it's real because you can feel that pain moving up and down your face.

Don't be a doubter. John chapter 3 verse 18 tells us that those who believe in Him is not condemned but those who do not believe is condemned already, because they have not believed in the name of the only begotten Son of God. I know God is real and I know that Satan is real too. I also know that Satan is trying to keep people who don't believe in God from coming to the realization that God does exist.

There is a saying that a lie will complete laps around a town before the truth even have a chance to tie its shoelace. God is real. Read His word, the Bible, with an open mind and you'll find out the truth.

Prayer & Encouragement

Lord may someone come to know You after reading this passage. Let them know You are real. Open their eyes that they may see You at work In Your name we pray. Amen!!!

Pray that the God you do not believe exist
right now will reveal Himself to you somehow.
Once you believe, you will have no regrets.

We Are His

For all who are led by the Spirit of God are sons of God.
– Romans 8:14

Wow! We're sons of God. Created in His image after His likeness. We're sons of the King of kings. We are princes. Better yet, we have been crowned kings by Him and anointed priests (Rev. 1:6). Our kingdom is not of this world for we're in this world but not of it (John 15:19). When we accepted Jesus as our Savior and Lord and invited Him to come and dwell in our hearts, the Holy Spirit (the Spirit of Christ) came inside us and have been comforting us, guiding us, leading us and taking care of us in every way possible. It is the Holy Spirit who will raise us up (those whose bodies go to sleep in Christ) immortal on the Lord's Day (Romans 8:11). The foregoing may be a little deep for some Christians. It is good to discover the truth. Study His Word so that no one misleads you.

Prayer & Encouragement

Father, thank you for making us your sons. And not only sons but joint heirs with Jesus (Romans 8:17) whereby we are partakers of everything Jesus has. Thank you Abba. Father, Amen. It's time to keep shouting praises to our God continuously (Psalm 34:1). We cannot thank Him enough for Taking away from us what we deserve (death) through His great mercy and giving us what we do not deserve (abundant and eternal life) through His grace.
THANK YOU DADDY!!!

Our Audience of One

And in the process of time it came to pass, that Cain brought of
the fruit of the ground an offering unto the Lord. And Abel, he
also brought of the firstlings of his flock and of the fat thereof.
And the Lord had respect unto Abel and to his offering.
But unto Cain and to his offering He had not respect.
– Genesis 4:3-5

Hosanna, blessed are You O Lord our God, Hosanna in the
highest. Lord You deserve the highest praise, Hallelujah! We
give You our best today because You deserve the best. Lord we
remember how Abel gave You His best and received not only
Your richest blessings but Your highest commendations and we
remember David, a man after Your own heart getting all the raw
materials for the building of Your house prepared in abundance.
Before he died he made sure his son Solomon had everything
he needed to build the temple -an enormous quantity of gold,
silver, bronze, iron, timber, stone, and skilled craftsmen. 1
Chronicles 22:14-15

Whatever we do, let us do our best
for our audience of one.

Prayer and Encouragement

Lord thank You for receiving from us just what we are able
to do which is our best and adding your super to our natural.
In Jesus name, Amen. Whatever you do for God,
Give it your best.

The Complete Work
of Our Savior

How blessed is he whose trespasses has freely been forgiven. Whose sin is totally washed away, by the blood of Jesus Christ and now stands holy, before the sight of heaven.

When Were Forgiven, No Record
Is Kept of Our Past Failures

17 For if by one man's offence death reigned by one; much more they which receive abundance of grace and of the gift of righteousness shall reign in life by one, Jesus Christ.)

18 Therefore as by the offence of one judgment came upon all men to condemnation; even so by the righteousness of one the free gift came upon all men unto justification of life.

19 For as by one man's disobedience many were made sinners, so by the obedience of one shall many be made righteous -Romans 5:17-19

Prayer and Encouragement

Thank You for Your perfect work
of salvation for the fallen human race Lord.
As by one man's (Adam) sin death came into
the world even so by one man's (Jesus)
obedience of one shall many be made righteous.

Stand Up And Tell Me If You Know My Jesus!!!

He knew the wretch I would be, yet He loved me.

While He was on the cross each of us was on His mind. That is why I can join with all those in His family who have been washed in the fountain and cleansed by His blood and say, Amazing grace how sweet the sound that saved a wretch like me. I once was lost but now I'm found, was blind but thank God I now can see.

> I know He loves me and
> that is the reason I love Him
> Because He first loved me

Jesus is the lover of my soul. Jesus is the healer of my sin sick soul. Jesus is the deliverer of my oppressed and captive soul. Jesus is the Author and Finisher of my faith. That is why I love Him so, Jesus is my all in all.

Prayer and Encouragement

Jesus I'm in love with You my Lord and my Savior.
There is none other but You. There is none like You.
My Jesus I'd rather to have You than anything this
whole world has to offer me. If you don't love Him,
you don't know Him get to know Him.

When There's an Encounter with God

You know, Jacob wrestled with God and came away from
that encounter changed forever. His name was changed from
Jacob (sup planter, trickster) to Israel (prince who wrestled
with God and man and prevailed). He changed
the name of the place where he and God wrestled,
to Peniel which means "face of God".
– Genesis 32:30

Each of us needs our own "Peniel," a place to meet with God,
wrestle with Him and come away changed.

God has given us just such a place -the Bible. In His Word
we can meet Him, get to know Him and come away forever
changed.

In the Bible we have the awesome opportunity to meet God
face-to-face! He tells us who He is and what He wants from us
and even divulges His plans for us (Luke 16:27-31).

Prayer and Encouragement

Lord teach us to stay in your Word and the benefits
from this practice as You taught Joshua. Amen!
When in your life have you "wrestled" with God and
come away changed? He's with us in every challenge.

God Restores

I will restore to you the years that the swarming locust
have eaten, the crawling locust, the consuming locust,
my great army which I sent among you .
– Joel 2:25

After getting saved I remained fully devoted to my Faith for the first two years then straddled the fence for the next nine following years to the extent that my brothers and sisters in the Lord would say I've backslidden. I agreed and in the year following that nine years of wandering I restored my fellowship to the Lord.

After returning to the Lord, I quickly found out that God never moved away from me during what I call that "dark" period of my life (the nine years straddling the fence). God's word is true and the scripture which says, "When an unclean spirit goes out of a man, he goes through dry places, seeking rest; and finding none, he says, 'I will return to my house from which I came. And when he comes he finds it swept and put in order. Then he goes and takes with him seven other spirits more wicked than himself, and they enter and dwell there; and the last state of that man is worse than the first." - Luke 11:24-26.

I was robbed of my innocence by this unclean during the "dark" nine years of my lifetime. But God in His great mercy and grace, has taken me back, cleansed me once more, has restored me to a position in Him just like "the prodigal son" (Luke 15:11-32) and He has never stopped restoring the years the swarming locust, the crawling locust and the consuming locust had eaten.

God will do the same for anyone who believes he/she can never return to God because of where his/her life is right now and

73

where he/she has been or God would never accept him/her after all that he/she has done.

God says anyone who comes to Him,
He will not turn away.

Come to Him just as you are and he will hug you, love you, clean you up and restore you. He says He's married to you (Jer. 3:14) and will not give up on you because you're His.

Prayer and Encouragement

Lord help us to pray for our brothers and sisters who've wondered away from you and help people to through some experience, return to you and realize all the blessings they're losing by staying away. We pray in Jesus' name. Amen.

If you knew the blessing that salvation brings,
you would never, ever stay away.

God is Always with Us

Eternal God is your refuge, and underneath
are the everlasting arms.
– Deuteronomy 33:27a

People are always going through some trial or suffering. Either they just came out of one or they're getting ready to go through another. Why? You may ask. Because, this is a world of sin and trials and sufferings are the result. No-one is trial free or free from suffering. Jesus never committed any sin and yet He suffered while walking this earth. He suffered more than anyone else ever did or ever will. He was tempted in all points just as we are, and yet still He never yielded. He understands our woes because He has been through, just like we are now, and He is with us. He does more than sympathize or empathize. He is right there with us bearing everything. He feels our every hurt and our every pain. God provides more than comfort for us in our trials and sufferings. He provides all we need to go through them and come out victorious as He stays with us in the midst of these trials and sufferings. Like He was with the three Hebrew men Shadrach, Meshach, and Abednego in the midst of the furnace (Dan. chapter 3). He is with us right now and He, the eternal God is our refuge, and underneath are His everlasting arms.

Prayer & Encouragement

Lord let us never lose focus of your presence in the midst
of any trial or suffering. Our God will never leave us
nor forsake us. He is our refuge and underneath
are His everlasting arms.

The Battle is the Lord's

Thus says the LORD, "Do not be afraid nor dismayed because
of this great multitude, for the battle is not yours, but God's"
– 2 Chronicles 20:15b

Have you ever felt like you're in a situation where everyone seems to be coming against or "attacking" you because you stood up for your belief in God and you know you're right.

You're not alone. As a matter of fact there are other Christians in other parts of the world who fear to disclose their beliefs because of reprisals, even from government officials in those countries.

This battle in the world is not ours says the LORD, but His. Trust Him to bring you through and out from these trials. He will fight these battles and all we need to do is praise Him in the midst of it. When we praise God in the midst of a battle, He will confuse the enemy into destroying themselves and you will not only gain the victory but will get all the treasures of the enemy. God is great and will take care of you better than you or anyone else could. Praise God!!!

Prayer and Encouragement

Lord, thank you for taking over all battles
I'm involved in and making them Yours.
Thank You that victories are guaranteed
when the battles are not mine but Yours. Amen.
Whatever battles you face, they're not yours but God's.

76

Who Can Be Saved?

For whosoever shall call upon the
name of the Lord shall be saved.
– Romans 10:13

Jesus did His work on Calvary's hill to fulfill the Father's plan and purpose. He prayed the night before asking the Father if there was some other way for His plan to be fulfilled please let it happen then. He said, "Father if it is possible let this cup pass from me." Then when He saw me and you and knowing how much we need a Savior in our condemned state, He said, "Nevertheless, not my will but yours be done father."

Grace and mercy spoke up from the depth of compassion, loving kindness, and tender mercy. He knew we didn't stand a chance. We owed a debt we could not pay and He was the only sinless, spotless, unblemished lamb that could pay this debt for us. One He did not owe. He loves us so much. O how He loved us, and loves us. At that moment heaven eclipse the earth like a sloppy wet kiss and the Vail of the temple rent in two opening up the way for everyone who wishes to, to come before the Lord God almighty without the intercession of priests anymore. For whosoever shall call upon the name of the Lord shall be saved.

Prayer & Encouragement

Lord we intercede for our brothers who do not know as yet that they can call upon You and be saved. May doors be open in their hearts and clarity come to their minds, understanding that You will save whosoever call upon Your name. In Jesus name we pray. Amen. Let us stay in prayer continuously for our brothers and sisters who have not called upon the name of the Lord as yet. For we know our God is not slack concerning His promise but is longsuffering to us-ward; waiting for those who are to yet call upon His name and be saved.

Salvation

There is joy in the presence of the
angels of God over one sinner who repents.
– Luke 15:10

God provides redemption to any human being who will repent, believe and receive it. He says in His word that anyone who comes to Him He will not turn away. He loves us so much and doesn't want any one of us to perish. He states in John 3:16, "For God so loved the world that He gave His only begotten Son that whosoever believes in Him should not perish but have everlasting life." He also says he stands at the heart door and knock and if anyone opens to Him He will come in and sup with him -Revelation 3:20. Today if you hear his voice, harden not your heart and if you're going through something understand that you can call on the Lord while he may be found seek Him while He may be found. If anyone calls on the name of Jesus they shall be saved and their household also. Let nothing stop you from turning to the Lord. He is ready to receive you with open arms. He loves you so much. He wants you to have what's best for you and only he can give it to you. Accept Him today. You'll be very happy you did.

Prayer and Encouragement

Lord woo my brother to you as he reads these words on this page today. Woo my sister to You through the same process we pray in Jesus name. Amen. Accept Jesus as your Savior and Lord today. There is no need to put this off. It's the most important decision you'll ever make in your life.

God Saves, Heals & Delivers

He heals the brokenhearted and binds up their wounds.
– Psalm 147:3

I don't know about tomorrow. I don't know what tomorrow holds. But I know who owns tomorrow, and I know I'm in His hands. I'm not who I'm supposed to be or where I need to be but praise God I'm not what I used to be. Are you suffering from anxiety or depression? Are you unable to let go of past hurts? Have you been hoping or praying that the person who hurt you may suffer more than you do? You can release it all by giving it to Jesus. He says "Come to me all you who labor and are heavy laden, and I will give you rest. Take my yoke upon you and learn from Me, for I am gentle and lowly in heart, and you will find rest for your souls. For my yoke is easy and my burden is light." (Matthew 11:28). You may have suffered much and feel there is no way to get pass this hurt but God says not only will He deliver you out of all your hurts and lift you out of your depression but you shall have double the reward for your trouble (Isaiah 61:7). Whatever your situation, turn it over to the Lord, He's up all day and all night and never gets tired or overburdened with our cares anyway.

Prayer & Encouragement

Father help us to casts all our cares on You. You care for us. Amen. Brethren, be anxious for nothing but in everything through prayer and supplication, with thanksgiving, make your request known to God. And the peace of God which surpasses all understanding shall keep your hearts and your minds through Christ Jesus our Lord.
– Philippians 4:6-7

Healing is for Today

He was wounded for our transgressions,
He was bruised for our iniquities;
the chastisement for our peace was upon Him,
and by His stripes we are healed.
– Isaiah 53:5

Healing is here to stay until time wraps up like a scroll and opens into eternity where healing will not be needed as man will be in either of two places, heaven or hell. Healing will definitely no longer be needed in either.

God says, "My son, give attention to my Words; incline your ears to my sayings. Do not let them depart from your eyes; keep them in the midst of you heart; for they are life to those who find them, and health to all their flesh." -Proverbs 4:20-22. He further says in Proverbs 3:1, "My son, do not forget my law, but let your heart keep my commands; for length of days and long life and peace they will add to you." God lets us know in so many places in His written word that healing is here for as long as there is time. Here are a few- If you diligently heed the voice of the Lord your God and do what is right in His sight, give ear to His commandments and keep His statutes, I will put none of the diseases on you which I have brought upon the Egyptians. For I am the LORD who heals you. -Exodus 15:26. Bless the LORD, O my soul, and forget not all His benefits; Who forgives all your iniquities, Who heals all your diseases, Who redeems your life from destruction -Psalm 103:3,4a. He sent His word and healed them, and delivered them from their destruction. Psalm 107:20. He Himself bore our sins in His own body on the tree that we, having died to sins might live to righteousness - by whose stripes you were healed. -1 Peter 2:24.

81

Prayer & Encouragement

Lord, there are many who still do not believe healing is for today and tomorrow just as it was shown yesterday by Your Apostles. Help our unbelief. Amen.

Believe in the Lord and all His benefits for you. Stay in His word and in fasting and prayer.

Preach the Gospel

And this gospel of the kingdom shall be preached in all the world
as a witness to all the nations and then the end will come.
– Matthew 24:14

God has spoken and we are the ones to execute His command
upon this earth. Preach the gospel of the kingdom in all the
world as a witness to all nations, then the end will come. How
can they turn to a Jesus they do not know? How will they know
about Him without hearing about Jesus? How will they hear
if no-one preaches to them? How can someone preach unless
he/she is sent? Faith or believing in Jesus comes by hearing
the word of God preached. So preach the word instantly in
season and out of season. Reprove, rebuke, and rebuff take
those hearing your message to repentance by making them
aware that they need a Savior to save them from their sins.
Preach the gospel and Jesus will do the rest. There is your part
and there is Jesus' part. We work together. Don't overstep your
bounds. Let the Spirit of Christ have his way.

Prayer and Encouragement

Lord help us to step up to our tasks
and remain within our bounds
when we do our duty. Amen.

Try to see every opportunity to preach the
gospel knowing Jesus is always with us.

The Great Commission

All authority has been given to Me in heaven and on earth.
Go therefore and make disciples of all nations, baptizing
them in the name of the Father, and of the Son, and of the
Holy Ghost, teaching them to observe all things that I have
commanded you and lo, I am with you always,
even to the end of the age. Amen.
– Matthew 28:18-20

This is the great commission given by our Lord and Savior Jesus Christ after His resurrection and just prior to His ascension to heaven. In the Old Testament a commission is given by the Father to the children of Israel through His servant Joshua in Chapter one of that book.

Prayer and Encouragement

Lord help us to obey Your command and carry out
Your commission with strength and courage. Amen.
He's provided everything we need to
fulfill His great commission to us
- Lo, He's with us always, even to the end of the age.

His Mission is the Same Today as Before

For the Son of Man has come to seek and to save that which was lost.
– Luke 19:10

He started His ministry preaching or proclaiming that the kingdom of heaven is here. Everywhere He went He preached and taught the word to the people demonstrating such love and compassion that had never been seen before. He turned water into wine at a wedding reception when the groom ran out of wine. He fed five thousand with five loaves of bread and two fish. He healed everywhere He went. The blind saw, the deaf heard, the dumb spoke, the crippled got up and walked, lepers were cleansed, the dead arose and many other miracles were done by Him. He did all this to show the world that the Son of Man was here "tabernacle" with men. Then He promised that the works everyone sees Him doing His followers will do also. Even greater works would be done by them. - John 14:12. He told us just before leaving after His resurrection that these signs shall follow His disciples (those who believe) who are you and I, In His name they will cast out demons, they will speak with new tongues, they will take up serpents and if they drink anything deadly it will by no means hurt them, they will lay hands on the sick and they will recover. (Mark 16:17-18).

Prayer & Encouragement

Lord help us to carry out your mission successfully.
Help us to lift You up Lord so souls may be drawn to You.
Amen. He came to seek and to save that which was lost.
His mission has not changed and we are to do the works
that He did and even greater according to His word.

Have You Tried Him?

Oh taste and see that the Lord is good,
blessed is the man who trusts in Him.
– Psalm 34:8

The Lord is merciful and gracious toward us. He is slow to chide and swift to bless. He looks beyond faults and ministers to the needs of His people. He is almighty, victorious, the Lord of hosts. He takes care of our every need. He deserves all the glory, honor, praise, worship and adoration. He is God all by Himself and besides Him there is no other. He is the only true and living God. And we could go on and on as His attributes are infinite. Have you tried Him? Do you know Him? He knows you from the inside out better than you know yourself. He knew you before you were formed in your mother's womb. -Jeremiah 1:5. This may sound unbelievable but He knew everything that would happen in your life up to this point while you're reading this devotional and beyond. Yes He knows your future. And He set this moment up as a divine appointment for Him to work a marvelous work in you right now. Oh taste and see that the Lord is good. Blessed you'll be if you trust in Him right now. He loves you more than anyone else on this earth does and where others you were depending on has failed you He will not. He will come through for you. Just give Him that chance to take care of you (Matthew 11:28-30; 1 Peter 5:7).

Prayer & Encouragement

Father we pray for our brothers and sisters who don't know you in the pardon of their sins today that they will soon. Give Jesus a chance in your life today. 2 Corinthians 6:2
You'll be amazed by the transformation
that begins immediately.

86

You May Be the Only Bible

Let your light so shine before men that they may see your moral
excellence and your praiseworthy, noble and good deeds and recognize
and honor and praise and glorify your Father Who is in heaven.
– Matthew 5:16

As Christians we need to live up to who we profess to the world
that we are. The world is not reading Matthew, Mark, Luke or
John or any other book of the Holy Bible. The world is reading
us. We are the only Bible some people in the world will ever
read and so we need to be the light of the world our Lord Jesus
commanded us to be. Let your light so shine in the world. Be the
one to stretch a helping hand to someone who needs it. We've got
to be a little kinder and show a little kindness everywhere we go.
Shine our light for someone else to see. Then if we show a little
kindness, we'll overlook the blindness, of the narrow minded
people on the narrow minded streets of the world. Let us live
our lives to be the best, holy (separated to God), consecrated,
sanctified child of God we can be; even in the face of criticism
and humiliation from others. Our God will be more pleased with
us for so treated they our Savior. The world may hate you no
matter how much good you do. So what? You're not a part of this
world. Be of good cheer, Jesus overcame the world and so have
we. Continue to do good even to save just one out of the world.

Prayer & Encouragement

Father help us to be obedient to your command to let our light
shine no matter how we are being treated while doing
it as we ought to turn the other cheek when we get smote
on one side. Continue to do good. In spite of it all.
After all God is whom we are pleasing and His reward is
above our thoughts or requests.

God's Will for His Children

The Spirit of the Lord God is upon me. Because the Lord has
anointed me to preach good tidings to the poor. He has sent me
to heal the brokenhearted, to proclaim liberty to the captives,
and the opening of the prison to those who are bound.
– Isaiah 61:1

It's our Father's will for all his children to preach good tidings
to the poor, to heal the brokenhearted, to proclaim liberty to
the captives, and open the prison for those who are bound. This
can only be done through Jesus Christ as we can do all things
through Him who strengthens us (Phil. 4:13). Our God requires
this from us collectively in addition to our individual work
according to our gifts given to us for the benefit of the body
of Jesus, the church. In Luke 4:18 Jesus taught from this same
verse -Be anointed to teach the gospel to the poor (Salvation);
to heal the brokenhearted (emotional wholeness); to proclaim
liberty to the captives (freedom); and recovery of sight to the
blind (healing). Then He let us know that He's the vine, we are
the branches and Our Father is the vinedresser. If we are not
connected to Him in this life, we will be gathered and thrown
in the fire and burned.

Prayer and Encouragement

Lord help us to fulfill your perfect will for our lives.
Help us to stay connected with You Lord. Help us to take
the time necessary to build our relationship with You Lord.
Help us to teach and preach Your Word with power,
strength, clarity, compassion and empathy. Amen.
We must will to do His will.

When the Time Is Right

"But when the fullness of the time had come,
God sent forth His Son, born of a woman, born under the law, to redeem
those who were under the law, that we might receive the adoption as sons."
– Galatians. 4:4-5

God does nothing before the time.

He loves us so much that He will turn up late (in our eyes) when
we desperately need Him (John 11). A songwriter says, "He may
not come when we want Him, but He'll be there right on time.
Because He's an on time God, yes He is." There has been some
moments in my life when He showed up late (in my eyes) but
when He did He took care of the matter and everything was
alright thereafter.

Prayer and Encouragement

Lord thank you for showing up especially when in our eyes
You were running late. Thank You for helping us to
understand (through your actions) that You showed up just at
the right time. Trust in the Lord and whatever He promised. It
may seem to be taking such a long time that you may think
He either forgot or changed His mind. God never does any of
those. He never forgets and never goes back on His word. If
He said that He would do it, it will SURELY come to pass.

Having an Understanding of the Times

The sons of Issachar had understanding of the times,
to know what Israel should do. Their chiefs were 200.
All their brethren were at their command.
– 1 Chronicles 12:32

To have an understanding of the times, understand 3 factors
1. Culture: Understand the people & the place where you live.
2. Timing: Understand the times & discern when to move....
3. Strategy: Know what to do & the steps to take.

If anyone lacks wisdom let him ask
God who gives to each liberally.

Once one is able to understand the times and the events going
on in his/her life there will be success. God is ready willing and
able to guide if asked. Ask, seek, and knock.

Prayer & Encouragement

Heavenly Father, help us to be totally yielded to You Lord.
Yield to the Lord so He can take over your life today.

The Last Days

And afterward I will pour out my Spirit upon all flesh;
and your sons and your daughters shall prophesy, your old men
shall dream dreams, your young men shall see visions.
– Joel 2:28

In the last days. These are the last days. These days started after the death of Christ and our days are being referred to as the last of the last days. Our sons and daughters have been prophesying for ages, our old men have been dreaming and our young men have been seeing visions. Just where are you in all this last days experiences?

If you haven't accepted Jesus as Lord and Savior as yet, you're missing out on a lot. Make use of this opportunity now and pray this prayer...

Prayer and Encouragement

Father, I am a sinner and I am sorry for my sins. I am asking You to forgive me. By faith I receive Jesus Christ as my Lord and Savior. I now believe that I am saved. Thank You Father. In Jesus' name. Amen. You may feel nothing like sparks or supernatural experience because all you need is God's word of assurance that you're saved and now His child. Find a church home and attend church services regularly while reading your bible and praying to God, your Father, daily. God Bless You!!!

Spiritual Warfare

For though we walk in the flesh, we do not war after the flesh:
(For the weapons of our warfare are not carnal, but mighty
through God to the pulling down of strong holds;
Casting down imaginations, and every high thing that exalteth
itself against the knowledge of God, and bringing into
captivity every thought to the obedience of Christ...
– II Corinthians 10:3-5

This is a spiritual warfare we're in and we cannot for one second let down our guard. For we know that the enemy goes to and fro roaming this earth as a roaring lion seeking whom he may devour. Therefore let the mighty strength of the Lord make you strong. Put on the whole armor of God so you can defend yourself against the devil's tricks. We are not fighting against flesh and blood (humans).

We are fighting against forces and authorities and against rulers of darkness and against powers in the spiritual world. So put on all the armor that our God gives. Then when that evil day comes, you will be able to defend yourself. And when the battle is over, you will be standing firm. Remember in the midst of every battle that no temptation has come upon you that is not common to mankind. God can be trusted and He is faithful to His word and to His compassionate nature not to let you be tempted and tried and assayed beyond your ability and strength of resistance and power to endure. With the temptation He will (always) also provide a means of escape or a way out that you may be capable and strong and powerful to bear up under each trial patiently.

Finally, with this whole armor of God, that is, the breastplate of righteousness, the helmet of Salvation, the belt of truth, the footwear of the gospel of peace, the shield of faith, the sword of the spirit which is the Word of God and prayer, keep in mind that though we walk in the flesh, we're not carrying on our warfare according to the flesh and using mere human weapons here.

The weapons of our warfare are not physical, but they mighty before God for the overthrow and destruction of strongholds. We refute arguments and theories and reasoning and every proud and lofty thing that sets itself up against the true knowledge of God; and we lead every thought and purpose away captive into the obedience of Christ (the Messiah, the Anointed One).

Prayer & Encouragement

Father let us not confuse our duty in Your Kingdom
nor let our guard down at any time. Amen.

Be encouraged, our heavenly Father has
everything covered for us in this
spiritual warfare we are facing.

Put On the Armor and Stand Firm

Put on the whole armor of God that you may
be able to stand against the wiles of the devil.
– Ephesians 6:11

A lady doesn't put on a formal dress and prada to go play tennis on the tennis court and a gentleman does not dress in football gears to go to a black tie affair. No, they would be wrongly dressed, out of place and probably laughed at. It's no different in the spirit realm. You cannot stand before the enemy half-dressed or in the wrong clothing with the wrong weapons, or right weapons held improperly. You would be laughed at as the enemy sees you are unprepared and the battle is already in his favor. Make sure you're dressed properly for battle at all times when fighting the devil as he and his "henchmen" are always waiting for a moment of weakness to strike at you."

We do not wrestle against flesh and blood, but against principalities, against powers, against the rulers of the darkness of this age, against spiritual hosts of wickedness in the heavenly places.

Therefore take up the whole armor of God so that you may be able to withstand in the evil day, and having done all, to stand. Stand therefore having girded your waist with truth, having put on the breastplate of righteousness, and having shod your feet with the preparation of the gospel of peace; above all taking the shield of faith with which you will be able to quench all the fiery darts of the wicked one. And take the helmet of Salvation and the sword of the spirit, which is the word of God; praying always, with all prayer and supplication in the Spirit, being watchful to this end with all perseverance and supplication for all the Saints." (Ephesians 6:12-18)

Prayer & Encouragement

Lord we want to be faithful and vigilante, persevering through everything and interceding constantly for the brethren. Help us and strengthen us to be everything we need to be in this spiritual warfare.

Put on the whole armor of God and keep it on at all times.

He Gives Us Power

Behold I give you power to trample on serpents and scorpions, and over
all the power of the enemy, and nothing shall by any means hurt you.
– Luke 10:19

He gives us authority over all the abilities of the enemy in this
spiritual warfare. We need not worry or fret in any situation.
He has given us the ability to overcome. We don't have to do
anything in the battles we face for they are not ours but His
really. It's great to know that as many as received Him, to
them He gave the right to become His children, to those who
believe in His name. Behold what manner of love our God has
bestowed on us, that we should be called His children. We are
of God and have overcome the enemy, because He who is in
us is greater than he who is in the world. We must go through
some suffering in this world of sin. Like Paul we can say God's
grace is sufficient to take us through. Therefore, glory in your
tribulations and sufferings knowing that God's strength is made
perfect in your weakness and nothing shall by means overpower
you. You are pressed on every side but not crushed, struck down
but not destroyed, always bearing in your bodies the mark or
strength of the Lord Jesus Christ. Through all our experiences
we are getting to know Him even more and more through the
fellowship of His suffering and the power of His resurrection.
Glory to God! Keep pressing for the mark of the prize of the
high calling which is in Christ Jesus knowing that after fighting
a good fight, finishing the course and keeping the faith, you
have a crown of righteousness, among great rewards to receive
on that great and glorious day.

Prayer & Encouragement

Lord let us never lose sight of the fact that we have all the power we need from you for the victory, because greater is He that is in us, than he that is in the world. Amen!

We have power over all the power of the enemy.
There's nothing to worry about.

Fasting and Prayer

I was fasting and praying before the God of Heaven.
– Nehemiah. 1:4

There are some things in this Christian walk which can only be achieved through fasting and prayer. –Matthew 17:21. In this spiritual walk, as Christians we have to let our spirit dominate the flesh. We have to walk in the spirit knowing that the law of the spirit of life in Christ Jesus has set us free from the law of sin and death. The spirit is at enmity with the flesh and vice-versa. It is our duty to mortify the flesh and one of the most effective way to achieve this is through fasting and prayer. During a period of fasting and prayer, the Christian is at his/her strongest in this Christian walk with the Lord. However, the Christian has to understand fully well, what the Lord requires.

Isaiah states the fast that the Lord has chosen for us is to loose the bonds of wickedness, to undo heavy burdens, to let the oppressed go free, break every yoke, share our food with the hungry, bring the poor who are outcasts to our house, cover the naked, and do not hide ourselves from those who need our help. Then our light shall break forth like the morning, our healing shall spring forth, our righteousness shall go before us, the glory of the Lord shall surround us, when we call the Lord will answer us and when we cry out He shall say, "Here I am."

Fasting and prayer requires acts of kindness and compassion. If you need more information to better understand, read the life of Jesus in the Gospels. His entire life is the epitome of fasting and prayer.

Prayer & Encouragement

Lord teach us how to please You through fasting and praying.
Amen. Learn how to fast and pray, then make it a lifestyle.

You will find new strength and realize your ability
to overcome the challenges of principalities
and powers of darkness.

Not By Might

Then he said to me, "This is the word to Zerubbabel:'not by
might nor by power, but by my Spirit,' says the Lord Almighty."
– Zechariah. 4:6

Whenever we are up against challenges (and we most certainly
will) the answer is not to try to overcome by our might nor by our
power (do not try to go up against anything in our own strength).
God is our refuge and strength, our very present help in the
time of trouble (Psalm 46:1), Success or victory will never be
achieved when we're up against the enemy of darkness except by
God's Spirit because it's not by might nor by power but by God's
Spirit. For over twenty years the children of Israel had postponed
the rebuilding of the temple to the point that everything they
tried to achieve in life was being hindered by their fear and
procrastination. Then God decided to explain and encourage
the leaders to gather the people and resume the building of the
temple so their blessings may be released. God chose Haggai and
Zechariah, His prophets to prophesy and encourage the people
of Israel to work. The task was finished so quickly and everyone
from other nations who opposed the work, were silenced. When
God gets ready to move nothing nor no one can stand in His way
for its not by might nor by power but by His Spirit.

Prayer & Encouragement

Lord teach us to trust and obey you in everything you require
of us as you know the effective way to get things done.
Amen. Does anything seem difficult or even impossible?.
Leave it in God's hands and just do what He tells you to do.
Our extremities are His opportunities and
our impossibilities His possibilities.

Faith Not Fear

For God did not give us a spirit of fear,
but a spirit of power, of love and a sound mind.
– 2 Timothy 1:7

Fear is the opposite of faith and where faith is there is no fear. If faith is from God then fear is from the devil and if God moves on our faith then the devil moves on our fear. The devil will try to get us to believe in his lies which develops fear and fear causes us to worry about things that have absolutely no impact on our lives or our future wellbeing. The solution is to pray rather than worry and the devil with his source of fear will flee from us. Draw nigh unto the Lord in prayer and He will draw nigh unto you. Then submit yourselves to God and resist the devil and he will flee.

Give no place to the devil. Remember, he is like a roaring lion seeking whom he may devour. The word of God says he is *like* a roaring lion not that he is a roaring lion. There is a big difference. You see, he has the ability to drive fear in someone if that person will allow him, but he is harmless. He roars but that's as far as his intimidation skills go. No further. Resist him when you submit yourself to God and he will flee. As far as defeating him totally goes, just build up your faith in God. Without faith it is impossible to please God for him that cometh to God must believe that He is and that He is a rewarder of those who diligently seek Him.

Prayer & Encouragement

God please keep reminding us that faith dispels
fear and prayer removes all worrying which
is the product of fear. Amen.

There is absolutely nothing to fear when you
believe in God. Perfect love casts out all fear.

No Evil Can Harm Us

No evil shall befall you, nor shall any
plague come near your dwelling.
– Psalm 91:10

Have you ever noticed that we go through many hardships in life both before coming to our Lord and Savior and since being with Him. The difference between before and after receiving Jesus Christ is His presence. He promised never to leave us nor forsake us. When you're up against the enemy you notice they cannot befall us for greater is He that is in you than he that is in the world. Sometimes the enemy may use people close to you or people in position of power to try to hurt you or try to destroy you but remember also, it doesn't matter how many there are against you or how much authority they seem to have, your Savior and Lord has all power.

The host that you can only see through spiritual eyes that are with us are greater in number and power than those we see with natural eyes who are against us. So there's no reason to fear or fret, God hasn't failed any of His children yet, and will never fail even one, because He can do everything but fail. There's none that has fallen from His hand, no, not even one. Therefore, be not dismayed whatever betides, God will take care of you. Beneath His wings of love abide, He will take care of you. No evil can befall you and no plague shall come near your dwelling for God has His plan in place and His army of angels surround you keeping you safe from all harm. He is the Almighty God and there's no other god like our God. None can dare defy Him.

Prayer & Encouragement

Lord, remind us continuously while going through any hardship or facing any opposition that You're with us. The enemy roars, but cannot bite. The enemy may send wild threats, but can never execute them because You're with us.

Your rod and Your staff comforts us. Amen.
Don't ever be afraid, our God is always with us protecting us so no evil can ever harm us.

Angels Watching Over Us

The angel of the Lord encamps all around
those who fear Him, and delivers them.
– Psalm 34:7

When Peter was sent to prison by King Herod, and his plan was to kill Peter, God's angel came and led him out of that prison to freedom. God's angel watches over us to deliver us in our time of need. We may not see God's angels but if we pray for our eyes to be opened we will see (2 Kings 6:17). We don't have to worry or fret. If we're falling God gives His angels charge over us to keep us in all our ways. In their hands they will bear us up, lest we dash our feet against stones (Psalm 91:11-12). God's angel helps to guide and protect us and are always at our beckon call. One angel is mighty enough to destroy tens of thousands. -2 Kings 19:35.

Never fear, we're so surrounded by God and
His angels that nothing can come against us,
His children, and prevail.

Prayer and Encouragement

Father, thank you for the way you have everything taken care of in our lives. We have no need to concern ourselves or worry about the plan or attacks of the enemy. We pray, knowing You will have your way. Thank You for Your angels who surround us and watch over us... Amen.
God and His angels are watching over us
every step of the way. Have no fear.

105

Angels

Bless the Lord, you His angels, who excel in strength,
who do His Word, heeding the voice of His Word.
– Psalm103:20

Angels. God's ministering spirits. They are engaged in all types of activities. Some bring messages of glad tidings, or announce special coming events; one wrestled with Jacob; while some are given charge over us, to keep us in all our ways, lest we dash our feet against stones.

All rejoice in the return
of a lost sheep to the fold
or a sinner who repents

They are here for us.
They are angels of the Lord who
encamp around those who fear God.

Prayer & Encouragement

Thank you for your angels Lord.

Be hospitable to everyone for sometimes
we could be entertaining angels.

The Power of Praying God's Word

Thy Word is a lamp unto my feet and a light unto my path.
— Psalm 119:105

Father in the name of Jesus we commit ourselves to walk in Your Word. We recognize that Your Word is integrity itself -steadfast, eternal, sure, and we trust our lives to its provision. You have sent forth Your Word into our hearts. We let it dwell in us richly in all wisdom. It does not depart from our mouths. We meditate in it day and night so that we may diligently act on it. Your Word is an incorruptible seed, abiding in our spirit, and it's growing in us mightily producing our nature, our lives. We thank You Father that Your Word is our counsel, our shield, our buckler, powerful weapon in battle. It is a lamp unto our feet and a light unto our paths. It makes our way straight before us, and we never stumble or fall for our steps are ordered by Your Word. We recognize the strategies and deceits of satan and we put a stop to them by speaking Your Word out of our mouths in faith.

We are confident Father that You are at work
in us both to will and to do Your good pleasure.

We exalt Your Word. We hold it in high esteem and give it first place in our lives. We boldly and confidently say that our hearts are fixed and established on the solid foundation -the Living Word of God. We pray that surely goodness and mercy shall follow us all the days of our lives and that we shall dwell in the house of the Lord forever. We see ourselves Lord, just as those who have come to You, and whom You will in no wise cast out. We pray Lord Jesus, that we have heard Your voice and that You know us, and that we follow You and You will give us eternal life and we shall never perish. We pray that we will not grieve the Holy Spirit of God, by whom we were sealed for the day of redemption.

We pray that You God who have begun a good work in us will complete it until the day of Jesus Christ.

We pray that Your faithfulness will establish us and guard us from the evil one. God, You're able to keep us from stumbling and to present us faultless before the presence of Your glory with exceeding joy.

Prayer and Encouragement

Thank You Father. I know that when I pray according to Your Word it will always be the right prayer. Stay in God's Word. It's total provision for us.

Twelve Benefits to Prayer

1. Prayer defeats the devil. (Matthew 18:18)

2. Prayer saves the unbeliever (Acts 2:21)

3. Prayer edifies the believer (Jude 20)

4. Prayer sends laborers into the harvest (Matthew 9:8)

5. Prayer heals the sick (James 5:13-15)

6. Prayer overcomes the impossible (Matthew 21:22)

7. Prayer changes the natural (James 5:17, 18)

8. Prayer brings the right things to pass (Matthew 7:7-11)

9. Prayer imparts wisdom (James 1:5)

10. Prayer brings peace (Phil.4:5-7)

11. Prayer guards against temptation (Matthew 26:41)

12. Prayer reveals God's answers (Luke 11:9, 10)

Prayer & Encouragement

Thank You Father for Your Word on prayer.

Praying God's Word

Jesus, You state that the world will know that we are Your disciples if we behave lovingly toward one another. Schisms, disputes, unkind criticisms and defamation of character are contrary to Your spirit.

Your love is a sacrificial love. John 3:16
It is unconditional love. Romans 5:8
Your love is constant and self-sustaining. Jeremiah 31:3

Lord we present our bodies as living sacrifice, holy and acceptable unto You for this is our reasonable form of worship. We also pray that we will not be conformed to this world, but be transformed by the renewing of our minds, that we may prove what is that good, acceptable and perfect will of yours. -Romans 12:1, 2. Your love provides for the best interests of the beloved, and You command that we should love one another as You have loved us. -John 13:35

We pray that we will be kindly affectionate to one another with brotherly love, in honor giving preference to others; not lagging in diligence, fervent in spirit, serving You, Lord; rejoicing in hope, patient in tribulation, continuing steadfastly in prayer; distributing to the needs of the Saints, given to hospitality. -Romans 12:10-13

Prayer and Encouragement

Thank You Lord. Your Word gives life. Amen.
When we pray God's Word
We pray His perfect will.

What Happens When We Pray

We pray, O God, that we shall serve You, the Lord our God.
– Exodus 23:25

We pray that we will fear You, the Lord our God, and walk in all Your ways and love You, and serve You, the Lord our God, with all our hearts and with all our souls, and that we will keep Your commandments and statutes which You command us today for our good. Deuteronomy 10:12-13. We pray that we do not turn aside from following You, LORD, but serve You with all our hearts. We pray that we do not turn aside, for then we would go after empty things which cannot profit or deliver, for they are nothing. For You will not forsake us for Your great name's sake, because it has pleased You to make us Yours. -1 Samuel 12:20-22. We pray that we will know You, God, and serve You with loyal hearts and with willing minds; for You search all hearts and understand all the intent of the thoughts. If we seek You, You will be found by us; but if we forsake You, You will cast us off forever. -1 Chronicles 28:9. We pray that we have been delivered from the law, having died to what we were held by, so that we should serve in the newness of the Spirit and not in the oldness of the letter. -Romans 7:6. We pray that we will serve You with gladness and that we will come before Your presence with singing. We pray that we will know that You LORD, are God and that it is You who have made us and not we ourselves. Psalm 100:2-3.

Prayer and Encouragement

Lord God speak to our hearts,
minds and spirit as we pray your Word today.
Praying God's Word moves Him to act in your favor.

Prayer of Love

And hope makes not ashamed; because the love of God
is shed abroad in our hearts by the Holy Ghost
which is given unto us.
– Romans 5:5

In Jesus' name we will make a fresh commitment today Lord, to live the life of love, to let Your tenderness flow through us and heal the wounded hearts of those we meet. Father, teach us to love even when things go wrong. To be patient and kind. To overlook the spiteful words of an angry person. To rejoice when someone at the office gets the raise that we thought we needed. Teach us to talk in love, to lay gossip quietly aside, and to take up words of grace instead. Lord Your Word says that Your love is already inside us. It has been shed abroad in our hearts.

Prayer and Encouragement

Today we resolve to remove every obstacle that would keep that love from flowing freely into the lives of others. We put resentments behind us and we forgive all those who have done us wrong. In the days ahead, cause us to increase and excel and overflow with Your love. Cause us to be what this world needs most of all, a living example of love. Amen.

Hope makes not ashamed; because the love of God
is shed abroad in our hearts by the Holy Ghost
which is given unto us.
Romans 5:5

Prayer

Our Father and our God, here we are once more before Your throne of mercy. God we just want to talk to our Daddy right now. We wish to see ourselves as your children who know very little in comparison to You. Grant us wisdom as You promised in James 1 verse 5, and grant it liberally we pray. We need You now our Lord, wait not just now but right now, God. If there was a time we needed You it's right now Daddy. There were times in our past life when we thought we could make it on our own and all we needed was self-confidence to make it in this life. But thank You God for the revelation before it was too late that we can't even walk without You holding our hands. Thank You for showing us that without You we can do nothing, without You we are nothing but with You we are the majority and we can do all things through You who strengthens us.God thank You for showing us that we are all part of Your body.

We are all members of one body, Your body, and we all have functions in Your body. Each having gifts given to us by the Holy Spirit in measure. The gifts are given according to where we are in the body and are for the sole purpose of building up the body of our Lord Jesus Christ. Thank you Lord for the fruit of the Spirit which just keeps on growing in us maturing us and aiding You in completing the good work You began in us that You are faithful to complete against that day of Jesus Christ. Lord thank You for the strength to complete this race as the cloud of witnesses are surrounding us with prayers of encouragement and strengthening as we cast off every weight and the sin that seem to so easily beset us. Thank You for guiding our eyes to stay focused on Jesus the author and finisher of our faith. Lord, oh that we may know Jesus in the fellowship of His suffering and the power of His resurrection. Knowing that we have been apprehended for that which is valuable and beneficial to us, we're forgetting all that is behind and reaching for that which is ahead. Pressing for the mark of the prize of the upward call of God which is in Christ Jesus. Help us our heavenly Father, never to miss the mark. For God our Father, if we should miss heaven our lives would be doomed and we don't want to share anywhere with doomed satan. Blessed assurance thank You. Jesus is mine and oh what a foretaste of glory divine.

We're joint heirs with You Jesus.
We're heirs of Salvation purchased by You.
Born of Your Spirit washed in Your blood.

Prayer and Encouragement

Lord We Thank You, Lord We Praise You,
Lord We glorify Your name!
Thank You Lord that we can call you anytime.

Pray Without Ceasing

Pray without ceasing.
– 1 Thessalonians 5:17

We should always pray so we don't faint (Luke 18:1), we should watch and pray less we fall into temptation (Mark 14:28) and pray with the knowledge that the effectual fervent prayer of the righteous avails much (James 5:16).

There is so much to gain or benefit
through praying to God often.

Prayer places one where the enemy can never come to. Prayer changes things and prayer changes the person praying as well. Prayer clears the mind of doubts, fears and anything that seem to cloud the mind. Prayer gives so much power both in the natural and spirit realms. Prayer is power we cannot live without. How is your prayer life? There can never be too much prayer. The more we pray, the closer we get to God and the farther we get from world systems which threaten our relationship with God. God never moves away from us, it is our actions that pull us away from Him.

Prayer & Encouragement

Lord teach us to pray and pray more than we pray right now. Stay in prayer. There's a lot more to benefit from praying without ceasing than we could ever imagine.

We Have an Advocate

If anyone sins, we have an advocate with the Father, Jesus
Christ the righteous. He Himself is the propitiation for our
sins, and not for ours only but also for the whole world.
– 1 John 2:1-2

Our God is love. When we invite Jesus in our hearts, the love
of God comes to live in our hearts and nothing can separate us
from His love (Romans.8:39). The rule and reign or the kingdom
of God is in our hearts (Luke 17:21) and we sit in heavenly
places in Him, Jesus Christ (Ephesians 2:6). When He ascended
He took His shed blood in a container to the mercy seat before
the Father which proclaims our redemption from the rule and
penalty of sin.

We have an advocate. Whenever we make a mistake (sin) here
on earth and a propitiation for our sins because each time the
tempter or accuser says to the Father see he/she just committed
another sin, our advocate and propitiation for our sins responds
by showing the nail prints in His hands and feet and the pierce
in His side and sweetly smiles and kindly says, "Behold, the
payment for his/her sin," and then points to the large vessel
before the mercy seat and says, "It's all under the blood." Glory
to God! Hallelujah!!!

As soon as we confess our sins, He is faithful and just to forgive
us and cleanse us from all unrighteousness (1 John 1:9). Also
read (Romans 8:1) Jesus takes care of it for us.

Prayer & Encouragement

Lord thank you for your assurance of Your plan at work
in us and help us to run to You each time
we fail You and not from You. Amen.

Be like David, the man after God's own heart. It doesn't
matter how "grave" or how often the sin, run to God for
forgiveness and restoration. The righteousness in a righteous
man is that each time he falls, he gets back up again.

It's Prayer Time!

Father in the name of Jesus we're coming before you on behalf of everyone reading this book. Lord we lift up each person to You, God. You know each one by name and by number. We dedicate them to You Lord and ask Your blessing on each one Lord. Even though we don't know everyone's situation, we're thankful that we serve an omniscient God and nothing is hidden from You God. Touch each person Lord because we surely need a touch from You.

Breath of life breathe upon us now we pray. Keep Your hand of love and protection upon us Lord. Lead us, guide us & protect us from the evil one Lord. Keep us in Your care. Heal somebody Lord. Deliver somebody. Set somebody free from the devil's grip. In Jesus name we pray. Draw us closer to You now Lord. In Your presence is fullness of joy and at Your right hand are pleasures forevermore.

Father Wash us in the cleansing blood of Jesus Christ and strengthen us for this journey God. We need You Lord. Be a lamp unto our feet and a light unto our path for these last and evil days we're now living in Lord. These are perilous times Lord and if there was ever a time we need You God it is now.

Lord pour Your oil of anointing on Your children's heads right now Lord and grant us all that we stand in need of for this Journey O God we pray. Be with us now O God. We pray in the mighty name of Jesus and say Thank You Sir, Amen!!!

Father we're coming before Your throne in the name of Jesus. We pray that we will be strong in You, Lord, and in the power of Your might. We put on the whole armor of God, that we may be able to stand against the wiles of the devil. For we do not wrestle against flesh and blood, but against principalities, against powers, against the rulers of the darkness of this age, against spiritual hosts of wickedness in the heavenly places.

Lord we will take up Your whole armor,
that we may be able to withstand in the evil day,
and having done all, to stand.

We pray that we will stand therefore, having girded our waists with truth, having put on the breastplate of righteousness, and having shod our feet with the preparation of the gospel of peace, above all, taking the shield of faith with which we will be able to quench all the fiery darts of the wicked one.

We pray also that we will take the helmet of salvation, and the sword of the spirit, which is the word of God, praying always with all prayer and supplication in the spirit (Eph. 6:10-18). Amen.

Prayer and Encouragement

God we thank You and we praise You.
Help us to grow strong spiritually.
Open our eyes that we may see the way
we should go. Teach us how to use the weapons
of our warfare. Teach us how to pray and
praise you until we breakthrough!!!

God is on our side.
We are victorious!!!

Someone Needs Prayer Right Now

Someone had a rough night and is thinking of the unthinkable this morning. Someone is asking, "Why doesn't God just take me now? I can't take this anymore!" Pray my brother. Pray my sister. Cry, weep, and mourn if you have to. God understands every tear. Be Encouraged. The songwriter says, "I just can't give up now. I've come too far from where I started. Nobody told me, the road would be easy. I don't believe He brought me this far, to leave me." Jesus is only a prayer away. He promised never to leave us or forsake us. We're praying for you. God bless you.

Prayer and Encouragement

Father in the matchless name of Jesus we're coming before
You on behalf of our brothers and sisters who are
discouraged right now. Lord we don't know the situation
they're going through but You do. That is why You have laid
it on our hearts to intercede at this time. Lord. We pray for an
anointing on these our brothers and sisters that will destroy
every yoke of bondage in their lives Lord. We pray Your
power and Your glory will come down upon them Lord.
Strengthen them Lord. Lead them to Your word Lord.
Your Logos which will become Rhema in their hearts Lord.
Let Your word encourage, comfort and edify Lord.
Send someone to be an angel of help to each one Lord.
We will continue in prayer after closing this one Lord.
We pray in the mighty name of Jesus. Amen!!!
Thank You Lord for being the lifter of my head.
Jesus is only a prayer away and
He will fix everything when you ask Him.

120

Afternoon Prayer

O Lord our God how majestic is Your name in all of the earth. You have made the earth, moon and the stars. The sun and all the galaxies. You shaped and fashioned all the planets and put them in their rightful position You made all inhabitants on the earth. All that make up each planet and the elements in the various spheres are created by You Lord and You rule them all.

O Lord our God how majestic is your name in all the world. Lord You spoke light into darkness and the darkness was dispelled. You later made a greater light to rule the day and a lesser light to rule the night. You separated the night from the day and the waters under the sky from the waters above it. You separated the waters under the sky from the dry land and called it earth. You made the trees and the shrubs and the flowers and the fruit with its seed. You made the beast of the fields and the domestic animals that walks upon the earth. You oh Lord made the crawling animals, the fowls of the air, the fish and creatures of the sea.

O Lord our Lord how majestic is Your name in all the earth. When I look at the beauty of Your creation here on earth and throughout the galaxies, I am amazed at a God like You and the fact that You take the time to be mindful of me. Little insignificant me who is of much less importance than the duties of caring for all the splendors of this world, separate and combined.

No one man nor this entire earth's population collectively could take on the responsibility of caring for this universe. The heavens declare Your glory God and the firmament shows your handiwork. Lord You are magnificent! Lord You are glorious!

Lord You are wonderful! Lord You are marvelous! O Lord our Lord how majestic is Your name in all the earth.

Prayer and Encouragement

Lord You are bigger than any thought, task or imagination. Thank You for taking the time to look down on each and every one of us. Amen. If you have a voice, take time to thank God. In everything give thanks.

The Power of Our Prayers

I exhort, therefore, that, first of all, supplications, prayers,
intercessions, and giving of thanks, be made for all men; for
kings, and for all that are in authority; that we may lead a
quiet and peaceable life in all godliness and honesty.
– 1 Timothy 2:1-2

God has called us to intercede for everyone. He has commanded us to pray for those in authority. He has given us His Word, His power, His Name, His authority and His faith. We have all the tools necessary to pray effectively for our government and its leaders. We need to intercede. It is our responsibility as believers to get involved in the affairs of our country. We did not choose the Lord, He chose us. He personally selected each of us. He called us out of our own plans for our lives and out of the confusion of our past. He called us into the excellence of His kingdom, into communion with Him and into His plan for our lives. It may sometimes seem that the plan lies just around the next bend in the road of our spiritual walk with Christ, just beyond our reach or not very well defined. But we "press on" so that we may grasp God's plan for us - the plan that God had in mind when He grasped us (Phil. 3:12). Let us keep moving on! His plan is there for us! And it is in His plan that we will find our firmest purpose, deepest fulfillment and highest joy. It is a part of God's plan to have people from all nations and the only way He will achieve this is through His ambassadors - you and I. Pray for the nations every day. Never underestimate the world changing power of prayers.

Prayer and Encouragement

Lord help us never to lose sight of Your plan for us which can only
be achieved through a close relationship with You. It keeps you
close to God while drawing others to Him through intercession.

Believe and Never Doubt

Believe in the Lord your God, and you shall be established;
believe His prophets and you shall prosper.
– 2 Chronicles 20:20

If God said it, just believe it.
Whatever He promised, He will fulfill.
He is the God who never forgets.
If He said He will do something,
it will surely come to pass. Believe and never doubt.

Let's look at some examples in the Bible of God fulfilling His promise. He promised Abraham that He would bless him with a son who would be born from his union with Sarah and would be the heir in Abraham's household. It took so long that Abraham and Sarah thought they would help God fulfill this promise by having a child through Sarah's maid Hagar (Sarah was barren).

God in His faithfulness blessed Abraham and Sarah twenty-five years after He made the promise to Abraham and still blessed the child born through Sarah's maid Hagar.

Joseph the great grandson of Abraham received a message from God through two dreams that his family would serve him Joseph, the son of his father, Jacob's "old age." After being sold into slavery by his brothers, serving time in prison for a crime he did not commit, some thirteen years later when he had forgotten about the dreams, God elevated Joseph to the second highest position in Egypt where he was sold into slavery. His family did come and pay obeisance to him.

124

The final example is God's promise to Abraham that after four hundred years of captivity in Egypt He would deliver Abraham's descendants and take them to the land Abraham was then sojourning on. After four hundred years of captivity in Egypt, God certainly kept His promise and raised up Moses to be used to by Him (God) to deliver the children of Israel out of Egypt. Is there something you know the Lord promised but it has been so long you wonder sometimes if He is still remembers or is going to do it? Believe that He still remembers and will do it. Never doubt God on His promises. A day in God's sight is like a thousand years and a thousand years is like one day. He doesn't forget. He never forgets. Even when men forget He doesn't. He is God.

Prayer & Encouragement

Lord let us never doubt or give up on any promise You've made to us. Help us to know Lord that You will never leave us nor forsake us. Help us Lord to keep moving forward and never look back. Help us Lord to know beyond a shadow of a doubt that Your peace that passes all understanding shall keep our hearts and minds through Christ Jesus. Help us Lord to trust You til we die. Help us Lord to hold on with an unwavering faith and belief in You. Trusting You Lord...
Amen.

Believe in the Lord your God and you shall be established; believe His prophets and you shall prosper.

Worshipping the Father in Spirit and in Truth

God is a Spirit and they that worship Him must
worship Him in Spirit and in truth.
– John 4:24

A teenager has just given birth to a child she does not know how to take care of. In secrecy she leaves the child on the steps of the father's parents. A woman takes her 16 year old son who has cerebral palsy to a center for daily care but this time doesn't return to pick him up. She'd had enough being a single parent. She loves her son very much but was at her breaking point. For the past ten years she has been working four jobs per week to make ends meet. Juggling a telemarketing job in the mornings during the week and a housekeeping job in the afternoons at a motel. Then getting up early on the weekend to work at a fast food restaurant and leaving there to get to the hospital for a part-time weekend job changing bedpans and mopping up hospital rooms, she had had enough. She just cannot go on anymore.

A woman has sought refuge in a home for "battered" women or to sugarcoat it, a home for victims of domestic violence. A child just ran away from a foster home because he/she is being mistreated. This child's parents were both arrested for drug possession and it's not the first, second or third time. The list goes on. Where does it stop? Where is the true help for these people in the world?

The places of refuge set up most times by people who had the same experience and was able to emerge victorious are the places most effective. Why? They've been there. They know exactly how it feels to be in those "shoes." They are the true worshippers who worship God in Spirit and in truth. When Jesus was here in the flesh He did the same and now He seeks anyone who is willing. He is there with those going through and He's there with those offering help in this present day and age. If you've been through some similar suffering and came out will you offer your services to help someone now going through the same? And if you are the one going through just say a prayer to God. It is simple. Just say, "God please help me!" He's only a prayer away.

𝒫𝓇𝒶𝓎𝑒𝓇 𝒶𝓃𝒹 𝓔𝓃𝒸𝑜𝓊𝓇𝒶𝑔𝑒𝓂𝑒𝓃𝓉

Lord there are so many people who need help in this world, to try to take on the task of being the answer would be overwhelming for any one person. Thank you for providing all the help needed Lord. For we can do all things through Jesus Christ our Lord who strengthens us. Amen.
Are you going through unbearable burdens right now? Help is only a prayer away. Have you been through some seemingly unbearable situation and came out victorious. Volunteer your service to a center that helps people going through a similar situation.
You'll be surprised at the blessings you'll receive just by being a listener or an advisor for just a couple hours per day or per week as you're able to. God Bless You!!!

The True Worshipper

God is a Spirit, and they that worship Him must
worship in Spirit and in Truth.
– John 4:24

You know we praise God for all He's done, all He's doing and all we know He will do for us. It's thanksgiving and praise. Thank You Jesus. Thank You Lord. Hallelujah! We give You the glory, the honor and the praise for all You've done and what You're about to do our God. We exalt You God. We lift up Your holy and righteous name because we know when we exalt You, when we lift You up; You will draw us to You. Draw us to You Lord Jesus, our God. That is praise and God indwells or inhabits the praise of His people. He doesn't just visit but He sojourns, He dwells, He lives there permanently. He will never leave us or forsake us. Now when we praise for a reasonable time in God's presence, we get ushered into the state of worship. There in His presence it is more than emotions flaring. It is more than a spirit of thanksgiving and praise. It is where we're not just thankful, appreciative or grateful for what's been done or what's being done but because we know who He is. We worship Him because we're aware that it is our duty. It is why we were created. So we worship in spite of... Lord even though I'm going through this situation right now, I know You're able. I believe You will. Even if I have to go all the way through and not be delivered out of this before, I give You my true worship in the name of Jesus Christ. I worship You God. I adore You God. I worship You God in Spirit and in Truth Lord! I will give You all my worship God, regardless of my situation.

Regardless of my circumstance I know who You are. I know You're the God that is in full control of all situations and circumstances not only on earth but in the entire universe. We give You all our worship because You're deserving of it Lord.

We worship You God! We worship You!
We worship Christ our Lord!

Lord we don't understand everything we go through and even when we pray for understanding and still don't see clearly even though you're showing us what we need to know, we're still going to worship you because You are still God. When You're the only one who can help and it seems the deliverance is delayed we're going to still worship because we know You are an on time God. Yes, true worshippers are who He seeks to worship Him. Be a true worshipper today.

Prayer and Encouragement

Lord, draw us to You and bring out true
and spiritual worship in us we pray. Amen.

Be a true and spiritual worshipper.
The Lord will seek you out.

My Soul Cries Out

When I remember the battles you fought for me. When I remember the victories You've won. When I recall all the trials You brought me through, that in my heart I can be strong. When I think of your goodness and all You've done for me, my soul cries out HALLELUJAH,

Thank You God for saving me.
Yes, my very soul cries out HALLELUJAH!
Thank You God for saving me.

You lead me beside the still waters, somewhere in the valley below. Then You pull me aside to be tested and tried, but in the valley you restore my soul.

My Jesus I love You so much. I don't know how, I just know I can never love You as much as You love me. I know I love You because You first loved me! I'm so glad to be a part of the beloved. I don't know why. I can't explain but this I know. I need You and You want my soul.

What does it profit me to gain this whole world
and lose my soul? Jesus, I'm Yours.

Prayer and Encouragement

Lord, I love You with my whole heart.
I yield myself to You.
When you surrender your heart to
the Lord you will never regret it.

Prayer of Praise

I will call upon the Lord, who is worthy to be praised;
so shall I be saved from my enemies.
– Psalm 18:3

The adversary cannot stand in the face of our praise. I will praise the Lord according to His righteousness. - Psalm 7:17 Praise is an act of the will. It is not merely an exuberance overflowing with words, but a self-induced declaration of thanksgiving - a sacrifice. The praiser chooses to praise. No matter what you may face today, offer a thanksgiving of praise in the midst of it. It is the best protection you can get.

I pray today our God that we will gird up the loins of our mind & be sober & rest our hope fully upon the grace that is to be brought to us at the revelation of Jesus Christ as obedient children, not conforming ourselves to the former lusts, as in our ignorance, but as You, God, who called us are Holy, may we also be holy in all our conduct. -1 Peter 1:13-15

Prayer and Encouragement

I pray that we will have the mind of Christ.
– 1 Corinthians 2:16
You've just got to praise Him.

Praise Is Who I Am

I will enter Your gates with thanksgiving and
into Your courts with praise.
– Psalm 100:4

When we begin to sing and to praise, the Lord will set
ambush against our enemies confusing and defeating them.
– 2 Chronicles 20:22

Rejoice in the Lord O you righteous!
For praise from the upright is beautiful. – Psalm 33:1

I shall not die, but live, and declare the works of the Lord.
The Lord has chasten me sore but has not given me over to
death. Open to me the gates of righteousness; I will go into
them, and I will praise the Lord. – Psalm 118:17-19

Telling to generations to come the praise of the Lord, and His
strength and His wonderful works that He has done.
– Psalm 78:4

There is none upon earth that I desire besides You.
– Psalm 73:25

Let us continually offer the sacrifice of praise to God, that is,
the fruit of our lips, giving thanks to His name.
– Hebrews 13:15

I will praise thee, for thou hast heard me
and art become my Salvation. – Psalm 118:21

You give us beauty for ashes, the oil of joy for mourning, the garment of praise for the spirit of heaviness; that we might be called trees of righteousness, the planting of the Lord, that You may be glorified!!! – Isaiah 61:3

Because Your loving kindness is better than life, my lips shall praise You. – Psalm 63:3

I will praise You yet more and more. – Psalm 71:14

Will You not revive us again, that Your people may rejoice in You? – Psalm 85:6

You are holy, enthroned in the praises of Your people. – Psalm 22:3

Prayer and Encouragement

Father we praise you with our whole heart, our lives. If we had ten thousand tongues praising you every second, that would not be enough from us. So we're thankful you accept what we offer not for Your benefit but to benefit us. Thank You Daddy. Amen!!! Praise the Lord while you have the chance and don't let anyone or anything hinder you. He's worthy, He's worthy, HE'S WORTHY!!!!

Praise Him While You Have the Chance

And Miriam responded to them. Sing to the Lord,
for He has triumphed gloriously and is highly exalted;
the horse and his rider He has thrown into the sea.
– Exodus 15:1, 20-21

Moses and the Israelites sang this song to the Lord, saying, I will sing to the Lord, for He has triumphed gloriously; the horse and his rider or its chariot has He thrown into the sea. Then Miriam the prophetess, the sister of Aaron, took a timbrel in her hand, and all the women went out after her with timbrels and dancing.

TRIUMPHANT PRAISE!!!!

Bless the Lord at all times.
Let His praise continually be in your mouth.
Let your soul make its boast in the Lord.

The humble shall hear of it and be glad. From the rising of the sun until the going down of the same, the Lord's name is worthy to be praised. O magnify the Lord with me, and let us exalt His name together.

Oh, I feel like praising Him. Yes I feel like praising Him. Praise Him in the morning, Ppraise Him in the evening, Praise Him at noon time, Praise Him all day long, yes I feel like praising Him. I'm gonna praise the Lord while I have the chance. Yes I'm gonna praise the Lord while I have a chance. If you don't want to praise Him don't hinder me. My God, My God, My

God, You're worthy of all the glory, the honor, and the praise and I'm going to praise You 'til I die.

Hallelujah! Hallelujah!! Hallelujah!!! HALLELUJAH!!!!!!!

Prayer & Encouragement

Lord I'm going to keep on praising You as long as there's breath in me. I lift my hands in praise and worship to You Lord. I pour out my heart before You. I worship and adore You Lord. I magnify Your holy name. I will bless Your name at all times. In the good times and those not so good times. I will give thanks and praise!!! As long as I live I will bless Your name. Yes, Lord!!! My soul loves You Jesus!!! Thank You Lord for a spirit of worship and praise today Lord. Amen.

Always Praise God

I will bless the Lord at all times,
His praise shall continually
be in my mouth.
– Psalm 34:1

I direct this devotion to people who are labeled "The Crazy Praisers" today. I know there is someone who has been in a service who doesn't care what anyone thinks when they get an opportunity to just go all out in praise to their God. Because when they think of His goodness and all that He has done for them. How they got into some traps and some snares that they didn't know how or when they got there and didn't see any way out but suicide sometimes. They would never consider suicide but there was just no way out of the predicament. Sometimes it was rock bottom and seeing no direction to go nor solutions to their problems But Jesus stepped in and made a way out of no way and had all the answers to the problems. Someone can relate to what I'm saying today. I'm talking to someone this morning who may be in such a situation right now. Whether you're in one right now or had been in such situation, SHOUT the praise to God. Dance a crazy dance like David danced before the Lord. Don't listen to what anyone has to say, this is your life you're desperately trying to save here. Dance, dance, dance, dance, dance, dance, DANCE!!! Keep on shouting while dancing, "Hallelujah, hallelujah, hallelujah, HALLELUJAH!!!" To God be the glory the honor and ALL THE PRAISE!!! I got my personal testimonies that make me want to shout every time I see how naive I've been, allowing the enemy to allure me into his traps and snares and EVERYTIME my God just keep on delivering me.

O how He loves me so much.
If I was the only one to die for
He would have still come.
Praise God!!!

Prayer & Encouragement

Thank you for the past I have. If I didn't,
I wouldn't have this praise within me that makes
me one of Your "CRAZY PRAISERS!"

Thank you so much for the life I now have in You
as a result of You delivering me over and over again
and never giving up on a wretch like me.

Bless all Your children today, both the prodigals like myself
and those born to parents in the House who grew up and were
nurtured in the House, remained in the House and
have never been immoral in their actions.

It doesn't matter how you started your life,
what matters is how you finish.

Praising the Lord at all times,
letting his praise continually be in your
mouth is one sure way to finish well.

Facing Challenges

It's a bright and beautiful day and my prayer today is that God will consecrate this day and our lives to His plans today. May this day be the best day our lives.

God bless everyone that reads this. Whenever we face challenges, we can go back to God's Word to discover and claim his promises. When we take them at face value, we learn to trust Him.

When we face uncertainty or difficult decisions,
the place to start is in conversation with God (prayer).

We need to keep walking, working, praying and serving.
He walks at our side and shows us
details as we go along life's journey.

Prayer and Encouragement

Lord please bring to our memory,
all we need to do when facing challenges. Amen.
Thank You Lord! There is nothing too hard for You!
You will always bring us through as we trust You.

Self-Control

A soft answer turns away wrath, but a harsh word stirs up anger.
– Proverbs. 15:1

Sometimes we disagree with someone and we use great emphasis when stating our disagreement. There are people who know to express their disagreement only through violence. It is important for everyone to know and practice the way most know how to express themselves when they disagree - remaining calm. If one person from the group of few who don't know how to, learns and begins to put this method into practice it will be well worth the trial. We are familiar with the term, "If the majority who know better does nothing to cancel the actions of the minority who don't, then it is just as bad as doing those negative actions along with the minority." Another popular saying is, "The negative actions of the few are so 'loud' they're drowning out the positive actions of the many." We need to teach by our actions. Start with a soft answer that turns away wrath before the harsh word we expect from these persons which will definitely stir up anger.

Prayer & Encouragement

Give us wisdom we pray Father, to teach those who need to be taught, how to dissolve conflicts even before they start, by example and any other way available to us. Lord, teach me how to speak a soft word. In Jesus' name we pray. AMEN!!!

Do something to help someone by
looking beyond faults and seeing needs.

I Corinthians 10:13

No temptation has overtaken you except such as is common
to man; but God is faithful, who will not allow you to be
tempted beyond what you are able, but with the
temptation will also make the way of escape,
that you may be able to bear it.
– 1 Corinthians 10:13

At times I see someone going through being treated unkindly by fellow brothers and sisters and ask the question which hurts more, stones or damaging words? Guess it's according to the way you look at it. Remember that saying? "Sticks and stones will break my bones but words can never hurt me." Well some people may disagree. This is the conclusion of the whole matter for me. Trust God to bring you through. He knows what's best for you and will never suffer you to go through more than you can bear. And the greatest thing in all these experiences is there's something good to learn and come from it. -Romans 8:28. Finally these experiences are here to make you strong. Let us stay in prayer for all our brothers and sisters regardless of what circumstances they are facing. Suffering produces endurance, endurance produces character, character produces hope, and hope does not disappoint us -Romans 5:3-5 (NRSV).

Prayer and Encouragement

Lord when life's circumstances challenge us, teach us to accept
Your direction. Help us to remember that all things work
together for the good of those who love You. Amen.
Be not dismayed, whatever be tide, God will take care of you.

Troubled? Turn To God's Word

I waited patiently for the LORD; and he inclined to me, and heard my cry. He also brought me up out of a horrible pit, out of the miry clay, and set my feet upon a rock, and established my steps.
– Psalm 40:1-2

Hear my cry O LORD; attend unto my prayer. From the end of the earth will I cry unto You. When my heart is overwhelmed, lead me to the rock that is higher than I. -Psalm 61:1-2. God is our refuge and strength, a very present help in trouble. -Psalm 46:1. No temptation has overtaken you except such as is common to man; but God is faithful, who will not allow you to be tempted beyond what you're able, but with the temptation will also make the way of escape, that you may be able to bear it. -1 Corinthians 10:13. The LORD is my light and my salvation; whom shall I fear? The LORD is the strength of my life; of whom shall I be afraid? When the wicked came against me to eat up my flesh, my enemies and foes, they stumbled and fell. Though an army may encamp against me, my heart shall not fear; though war may rise against me, in this I will be confident. -Psalm 27:1-3. I will say of the LORD, He is my refuge and my fortress, my God, in Him I will trust. –Psalm 91:2. No evil shall befall you, nor shall any plague come near your dwelling; for He shall give His angels charge over you, to keep you in all your ways. In their hands they shall bear you up, lest you dash your foot against a stone. You shall tread upon the lion and the cobra, the young lion and the serpent you shall trample underfoot -Psalm 91:10-13. Preserve me O God, for in You I put my trust. -Psalm 16:1. In You, O LORD, I put my trust; let me never be ashamed; deliver me in Your righteousness. Bow down your ear to me, deliver me speedily; be my rock of refuge, a fortress of defense to save me. For you are my rock and my fortress; therefore for Your name's sake, lead me and guide me. Pull me out of the net which they have secretly laid for me, for you are my strength. – Psalm. 31:1-4. Psalm 38. The Lord knows how to deliver the godly out of temptations and to reserve the unjust under punishment for the day of judgement. -2 Peter 2:9

Prayer and Encouragement

Thank You Lord that when I call on You
I know You will come to my rescue.

God is there for You. Don't doubt. Just Believe.

Rejoice In The Midst of Adversities

Blessed are you when men hate you, and when they exclude
you, and revile you, and cast out your name as evil, for the
Son of Man's sake. Rejoice in that day and leap for joy!
For indeed your reward is great in heaven, for in like
manner their fathers did to the prophets.
– Luke 6:22-23

This sounds like it could be the favorite verse of scripture for a great majority. As we read this scripture the thought comes to mind of the persecution and/or execution of the prophets of the Old Testament and the persecution of the early church. Deacon Stephen, the first martyr of this church era; James the brother of John, pierced right through with a sword; Peter, crucified upside down on a x-shaped cross; James, the half-brother of Jesus, cast down from a church steeple and then had his head bashed in with a club; Paul beheaded; and the list goes on and on. Some imprisoned for life, while others were stoned, whipped, thrown to wild beasts, sawn in two, beheaded or thrust through with sharp weapons. Still others were either exiled or thrown in boiling liquids or in later centuries burnt at the stake.

Given all of the above tortures and painful slayings of our brethren who openly professed their faith and never denounced our Lord Jesus Christ, there is still a method or strategy being used by the enemy, Satan, to use others in societies across this globe to persecute Christians which seems very dangerous, to God's people. I'm not talking about religions striving against each other or countries supporting one religion, going up against another country supporting a rival religion. But there is a subtle technique being used by our adversary the devil against God's people and he seems to think his strategy is working to stop the

143

advancement of God's kingdom. Even though through natural eyes, it seems to delay the work of God's children in advancing God's Kingdom, it's only a setup by God using the devil for His own purpose because the works of the Lord are in seasons or stages and some stages have to be completed in order for other stages to begin. Nothing in God's plan happens before the appointed time. Satan is trying to blind the eyes of the world from the truth and in doing so sometimes he uses the people who have this veil over their eyes to persecute the people of God for some other reason than their Christian faith. A mob rose up to stone Jesus and told Him "Not for any good works do we stone thee but for blasphemy." Yes indeed Satan has some in his psychological vice grip, using them for his filthy schemes. We're going to keep these people in prayer because they're still God's creation and only God foreknows them (Rom.8:29), as He did Saul of Tarsus. In the end God always wins. That's why we as Christians rejoice so greatly. We're on the winning side. Regardless of how it looks. We know the final outcome. We may seem defeated because a lot of us were executed in one way or another but wait until you get over on the other side because it's not over when God's people are killed. The body is asleep but the spirit and soul are safe in God's presence until that great day when all three shall reunite. At that time it will not be a corruptible body but a glorious body reuniting with the soul and spirit that will live forever with the Lord. Glory to God. His plan for us makes us invincible.

Prayer and Encouragement

Thank You Lord for Your infallible plan for us. Amen
Rejoice in the Lord always, and again I say rejoice.
He has made all things well.

Overcome Evil with Good

Love your enemies, bless those who curse you, do good to those who hate you, and pray for those who spitefully use you and persecute you, that you may be sons of your Father in heaven; for He makes the sun rise on the evil and on the good, and sends rain on the just and on the unjust.
– Matthew 5:44-45

That verse of scripture goes on to say,
"For if you love those who love you,
what reward have you?

Do not even the tax collectors do the same? And if you greet your brethren only, what do you do more than others? Do not even the tax collectors do so? Therefore you shall be perfect, just as your Father in heaven is perfect" (verses 46-48).

"Be ye perfect just as your Father in heaven is perfect." I believe, to get on the right track to becoming perfect or holy as another verse of scripture puts it (1 Peter 1:16) one should begin by seeking wisdom (Proverbs 3 13,14), and to gain wisdom one has to ask for it (James 1:5). The reverential fear of God is the beginning of wisdom. (Proverbs 9:10).

There was a young man who had a remarkable experience which I will partly "liken" to the parable of The Good Samaritan, the only difference in this young man's experience, I think, is that the person aided by him was known to him. Let me relate the experience and I'm sure you'll find it remarkably praiseworthy.

This young man was bullied by older boys in his neighborhood mainly because he didn't have an older brother (in this neighborhood, if you had an older brother you wouldn't get picked on by bullies). One day a young man tried to take his money from him, this was his allowance from his mother who was a single parent of four children. He resisted and was chased by the young man. He got away and shouted to his bully, "One day I'll grow up and be able to defend myself, you'll see. Just remember, David and Goliath." With that comment the boy ran all the way home.

He later learned that there is a God that says, "Vengeance is mine, I will repay."

And His word goes on to say, "If your enemy is hungry, feed him; if he's thirsty give him a drink; for in doing so you will heap coals of fire on his head.

Do not be overcome by evil
but overcome evil with good."
– Romans 12:19-21

Prayer and Encouragement

Lord, please help me to continually defeat evil with kindness.
In Jesus name. Amen.In the midst of adversity,
Everywhere Jesus went He did good.
Go and do likewise.

You Have Nothing to Be Ashamed Of

There is therefore, now no condemnation for those who are
in Christ Jesus, who do not walk according to the flesh,
but according to the Spirit.
– Romans 8:1

It doesn't matter what you've been through in your life or what you may have done before God. Once you repent and accept Jesus as your Lord and Savior, thereby living according to the Spirit and not the flesh, you have nothing to be ashamed about. The law of the Spirit of life in Christ Jesus has set you free from the law of sin and death. Don't let your past life hold you back. Walk in the freedom Salvation has put you in. Guilt and condemnation is a state of the mind that is in bondage; and as a convert the key here is to start working at mortifying the body and uplifting the spirit in you. By the mercies of God, present your bodies a living sacrifice, holy, acceptable to God which is your reasonable service. And be not conformed to this world, but be transformed by the renewing of your mind, that you may be able to tell what is that good, acceptable and perfect will of God. (Romans 12:1, 2). You can get pass your past. You can walk away from painful memories. You can stand upon the word of God. Let Jesus bring you pass your past so you can go on. He makes all things new. He makes all things perfect. Let Jesus who began a good work in you complete it for you. He never makes mistakes and He sticks to His word. Trust him and you'll have nothing to be ashamed of.

Prayer and Encouragement

Father we believe. Help our unbelief. Let us trust you by putting our hands in yours. You who still the water and calm the sea. You who walk on water and asks, "Is there anything too hard for me?" Amen.

Only trust Jesus to do it all right now.

Honest

You shall not circulate a false report. Do not put your hand
with the wicked to be an unrighteous witness. You shall
not follow a crowd to do evil, nor shall you testify in a
dispute so as to turn aside after many to pervert justice.
– Exodus 23:1-2 (NKJV).

The Contemporary English Version Bible rephrase this verse
this way, "Don't spread harmful rumors or help a criminal by
giving false evidence. Always tell the truth in court, even if
everyone else is dishonest and stands in the way of justice. And
don't favor the poor, simply because they are poor." -Exodus
23:1-2 (CEV) "Honesty is the best policy." This is a statement
I heard time and again while growing up. Another one is this
nursery rhyme, "Speak the truth and speak it ever. Cost it what
it will. He who hides the wrong he did, does the wrong thing
still."

God uses many different ways to get his message through to
us. He uses various communication techniques to indicate what
He requires of us and they are all similar, keeping the message
pure and undistorted. Whichever way is more understanding to
us, He knows it and delivers His message in that way. Of course
He's aware of the many different makeup and personalities He's
dealing with. So it is with the messengers. Whosoever accepts
the messenger accepts the one who sent the messenger so we
all have to be careful not to reject God because of a judgmental
attitude. God loves all of us equally and He shows no favoritism.
He is no respecter of persons and He is not a man that He should
lie. He says in His word "Be ye perfect just as your Father in
heaven is perfect." (Matt.5:48) I do believe He is including "be
honest" as your Heavenly Father is honest among all His moral

attributes He commands. All attributes making up or being under the umbrella word, "perfect."

Prayer and Encouragement

Lord help us to be honest in all our dealings regardless of the cost. Be honest in everything. God is with you.

Be Good

If it is possible, as far as it depends on you,
live at peace with everyone.

Do not take revenge, my friends,
but leave room for God's wrath, for it is written:
"It is mine to avenge; I will repay," says the Lord.

On the contrary: If your enemy is hungry, feed him; if he's
thirsty give him something to drink. In doing this you will
heap burning coals on his head. Do not be overcome by evil
but overcome evil with good.
– I Corinthians 12:17-21

Do not repay anyone evil for evil.
Be careful to do what is right in the eyes of everybody.
– Romans 12:21

Prayer & Encouragement

Father thank You for these Your words of wisdom to live by.
Thank You Lord that in and of ourselves there is none
righteous. No not one. Lord when we walk as You walked
and live as You lived what a difference it makes.

Thank You for Your Word (Your Instructions)
and Your Holy Spirit who teaches us, strengthens us
and helps us in every good work. For Your glory! Amen.
Be ye holy as He is holy.

Without Him we could not exist.
Without Him there would be no air to breath.

Use every breath of fresh air
you inhale to praise God.

In everything you say and do, Give Him praise!!!

Show A Little Kindness

But the fruit of the Spirit is love, joy, peace, longsuffering,
patience, kindness, goodness, faithfulness, gentleness,
and self-control. Against such there is no law.
– Galatians 5:22-23

Our Bible tells us that in the last days perilous times will come.
For men will be lovers of themselves, lovers of money, boasters,
proud, blasphemers, disobedient to parents, unthankful, unholy,
unloving, unforgiving, slanderers, without self-control, brutal,
despisers of good, traitors, headstrong, haughty, lovers of
pleasure, rather than lovers of God, having a form of Godliness
but denying it's power. From such people turn away! For of this
sort are people who creep into households and make captives
of gullible women loaded down with sins, led away by various
lusts, always learning and never able to come to the knowledge
of the truth. Now as Jannes and Jambres resisted Moses, so do
these also resist the truth, men of corrupt minds, disapproved
concerning the faith; but they will progress no further, for their
folly will be manifest to all, as theirs also was. -2 Timothy. 3:1-9.

This clearly tells us that in the last days the fruit of the Spirit
will be virtually absent from the people of the world unless the
members of the church (Christ's body) will remain the salt and
the light of the world so others will see our good works and
glorify our Father in heaven. According to legend, the Greek
philosopher Diogenes walked the streets with a lantern held
high, searching for an honest man. Whether he ever found one
is unknown.

Suppose for a moment there is a modern Diogenes, only instead
of seeking an honest man, a kind person is searched for. Joel
2:13 says: God is slow to anger and of great kindness. It's only

reasonable to suppose that His followers should evidence the same type of behavior. Now instead of being the Diogenes why don't we be the one to be found by these modern day philosophers in search of kind people.

Think about the kindness we have received from God and try to perform at least one good deed of kindness to a neighbor each day. Also, most important, remember who's our neighbor (see Luke 10:30-37).

Prayer and Encouragement

Lord in these last and evil days help us to glorify you and draw others to You through our works. Amen!

Be the one to invoke change in this world system.

The Magnitude of God's Love

For God so loved the world that he gave His only begotten Son that
whosoever believes in Him shall not perish but have everlasting life.
– John 3:16

The magnitude of God's love is way above our capacity to
fathom. God loves us so much. A songwriter puts it like this,
"If the entire sky was parchment and the oceans ink, were
every stalk on earth a quill; to write the love of God across the
sky we would run out of space or the oceans would run dry"
(paraphrased). God loves us even while we were disobedient,
rebellious, wretches, and in some instances, wicked. God
demonstrates His love toward us in that while we were still
sinners Jesus died for us. (Romans 5:8). Then when we accept
Him, see what an incredible quality of love He shows us that
we should be permitted to be named and called and counted His
children (1 John 3:1), then He makes us equivalent in position
with Jesus, being joint heirs with Him (Rom. 8:17).

Prayer & Encouragement

Lord thank You for Your indescribable love. AMEN!
With the rewards from accepting Jesus as your Savior and
Lord, no-one can make you feel inferior without your
consent. You are a child of a King. His royal blood flows
through your veins and His love for you far exceeds any
estimate, thought or imagination.

Oh How He Loves Us So

For God so loved the world that He gave His only begotten Son that whosoever believeth in Him should not perish, but have everlasting life.
–John 3:16

Oh, how He loves us so, oh how He loves us. He loves us so much. He loves us, oh how He loves us. He demonstrates His love for us by letting Jesus, His only begotten Son die for us while we were still sinners, and rebellious toward Him. Oh how He loves us. - Romans 5:8

Behold what manner of love our Father has bestowed on us to call us His children. 1 John 3:1. We do not deserve all these blessings for we are wayward sinners deserving only of death. But oh how He loves us so. Oh how He loves us. He loves us, oh how He loves us. Greater love has no man than this, to lay down His life for a friend. "A new commandment I give unto you," says the Lord, "That you love each other.

Even as I have loved you."
Oh, how He loves us so.
Oh how He loves us.

Prayer & Encouragement

My Father and my God, Thank you for your indescribable love. Oh what love, Oh what love....
The Father loves you so much. Take advantage of this great love today. If you haven't yet done so, repent of your sins and accept His Son, Jesus Christ as your personal Savior & Lord.

The Greatest of These Is Love

And now abides faith hope and love, these three,
but the greatest of these is love.
– 1 Corinthians 13:13

Now faith is the substance of things hoped for the evidence of things not seen. - Hebrews 11:1. This faith starts or comes by hearing God's Word. Romans 10:17. Having hope in God's promises for us is not wishful thinking but a sure hope built on Jesus Christ our sure foundation for fulfillment of these promises. They are sure. Our only hope is that we ourselves don't do something to delay or deny the fulfillment of these promises in our lives. The greatest of faith, hope and love, is love. For without love everything is meaningless. Fulfillment of God's purpose is based on our love. Our love endures long, is patient and kind. Our love should never be envious, nor boil over with jealousy, is not boastful nor vainglorious and does not display itself haughtily. Our love is not conceited, is not rude, does not act unbecomingly, does not insist on its own rights or its own way, for it is not self-seeking, touchy, fretful or resentful. Our love should take no account of evil done to it, not rejoice at injustice and unrighteousness but rejoice when right and truth prevails. Our love should bear up under anything that comes, be ever ready to believe the best of every person. Its hopes should be fadeless under all circumstances and endure everything without weakening. Our love should never fail.

Prayer & Encouragement

Lord please help us to have an unfailing love. Thank You Lord for showing us what true love is and how true love acts. Amen.

Have faith hope and love. Increase each with having love as the most important virtue.

The Greatest Commandments

So (Jesus) answered and said, "You shall love the LORD your
God with all your heart, with all your soul, with all your strength,
and with all your mind, and your neighbor as yourself."
– Luke 10:27

Many people in the world today
are wondering if God truly exist.

If all the things we see happening is recorded as worse now than
earlier times how can there be a God who allowed the world to
deteriorate like this? God is alive and is present everywhere.
He sees everything and knows everything. He doesn't intervene
because He gave man dominion over everything on earth. He
also laid down rules or commandments for man to obey and
all the commandments hang on these two, "You shall love the
LORD your God with all your heart, with all your soul, with
all your strength, and with all your mind, and your neighbor
as yourself." If you will obey these two commandments then
all the others will be obeyed. You may ask, "And who is my
neighbor?" The answer to that question is anyone you come in
contact with. We need to show love to everyone by being kind
thoughtful and considerate to them.

Prayer and Encouragement

Father help us to show love for you and our neighbors
as we show kindness to others. Amen.
Show love wherever you are, knowing you
may be the only Bible someone may ever read.

He Does Everything Out of Love

Then God saw everything that He
had made, and indeed *it was* very good.
So the evening and the morning were the sixth day.
– Genesis 1:31

It is a beautiful day filled with God's beauty and splendor for His children. This day is dedicated to the Lord's work as do His obedient children who are here to fulfill His purpose just for this day. That's what makes this day so wonderful. God and His children working together to fulfill His purpose for their lives thereby fulfilling their God ordained destiny. When everything goes according to God's plan this is a perfect world in His sight. Just for that moment. For we know who truly has dominion. Jesus Christ took it back from the devil who stole it from Adam in the Garden of Eden. Jesus is more than conquerors. He is the omnipotent God. The ruler of the entire universe. He gave up His glory to come to earth a tiny dot in the universe to save man, the inhabitant of the earth from the penalty of sin which man inherited when he gave dominion to the devil, that old serpent satan.

Prayer and Encouragement

Thank you father for giving us your son to save us from death and having eternal life (John 3:16). Thank you Jesus for completing the purpose you came here to when You uttered the words from the cross, "It is finished." You could have stopped at any time during your ordeal but for my sake and all others who accept the gift of eternal life, You didn't.

Thank You very much. The Holy Spirit did His part.
Because a dying soul was convicted on a cross beside Jesus
through His work, a soldier cried out "Truly Jesus is the Son
of God." Others there were convicted including
his brothers who doubted in the beginning.

Thank You Father, Son and Holy Ghost, for completing the
Salvation plan for mankind who You love so much. For all
You have done and continue to do, we are grateful.

Patience in Marriage

Perseverance must finish its work so that you may be mature
and complete, not lacking anything.
– James 1:4 (NIV)

Most of us, before we're married, imagine that love will solve
all our problems. But could it be that patience, more than love, is
the sum and substance of a great marriage? Our society rewards
problems solvers. Every challenge is an opportunity to be met
quickly. Then comes marriage, and we problem-solvers are
suddenly faced with a challenge that taxes the very essence of
who we are. We think we're called to fix things when they're
broken. To make things work. Then we wake up one morning to
find that the person next to us is more complicated than anything
we've ever had to deal with. It is two people who give expression
to marital oneness. Two people -usually polar opposites- who
commit themselves to building a framework for physical,
emotional and spiritual oneness, by accepting, respecting, and
unconditionally loving each other. To do so, however, takes time,
which means we have to be patient. It demonstrates the certainty
that what we hope for -physical, emotional, spiritual oneness- is
waiting for us, even though we can't yet see it. My wife and I have
had many years to practice the power of patience. Forgiving each
other. Acceptance. Instilling hope. The longer we're married,
the more practice we get. Every now and then even we married
veterans need to be reminded that oneness is an assurance that
only those with patience can hold on to -and one day realize.

Prayer and Encouragement

Lord, help us to know patience in marriage
works a lot like faith.

Husbands Love Your Wives

Husbands, love your wives, even as Christ also loved
the church and gave His life for her.
– Ephesians 5:25

A few of the verses before this one speaks to wives saying,
"Wives submit to your husbands, as to the Lord, for the husband
is head of the wife, as also Christ is head of the church, and
He is the Savior of the body. Therefore just as the church is
subject to Christ, so let the wives be to their own husbands
in everything" (vs. 22-24). The Lord laid out the order of the
family from the beginning of creation. Man was created and
the Lord said, "It is not good for the man to be alone. I will
make him a helper comparable to him." God then let a deep
sleep fall on Adam and took a rib, closed up the flesh and with
that rib made a woman and presented her to Adam. Adam said,
"This is now bone of my bone and flesh of my flesh; she shall
be called woman." Therefore shall a man leave his mother and
father and shall be joined to his wife and they shall become
one flesh. After the fall in the garden God then told the woman
she shall desire her husband and he shall rule over her (Genesis
3:16). Under grace dispensation Jesus says to love your wife as
He loved the church and gave His life for it. Love your wife as
you love yourself. This means to treat your wife with the utmost
respect. Husbands love your wives.

Prayer & Encouragement

Lord teach us how to love our wives. Teach us how to
honor them, respect them, care for them and protect them
just as Christ loves the church. Amen. Amen. Amen.
Husbands, remember that a happy wife means a happy life.

Wives Love Your Husbands

And the LORD God said, *It is* not good that the man should
be alone; I will make him an help meet for him.
– Genesis 2:18

I thank God continually for bringing my husband in my life. He
is a man of vision and prayer. He's tough yet he is gentle and
peaceful. He cares for me, protects me and respects me. He is
strong where I am weak. He loves his wife and his children. I
think a few of the things that hold us together as a couple are:
each of us having a personal relationship with the Lord, prayer
and the Holy Spirit. Whether your mate is saved or unsaved I
urge you to pray for him daily. Encourage him, laugh with him
and make sure to have time for just the two of you. Take time
to listen to his hopes, dreams, concerns and fears if he's dealing
with any. We as women love to talk. Men don't talk as much
so when he does come close and listen. I remember my mother
always saying – "When your father comes home let him relax."
I saw firsthand how my mother (a stay at home mom and busy
Pastors' wife) juggled so many responsibilities but always made
time to put her husband first and minister to him. That was a
blessing and good training.

Prayer and Encouragement

Lord, help me to be a good wife. Help me not to be a nag but
an encourager. Help me to speak to the king inside of my
man. Help me Lord to build him up and not tear him down.
Help me to be his confidant and a safe haven.
A good marriage is hard work but worth it!!!

He Can Heal a Broken Heart

Hear my cry, O God; listen to my prayer. From the ends of
the earth I call to you, I call as my heart grows faint;
lead me to the rock that is higher than I.
– Psalm 61

Your heart has been broken. Your have cried til your eyes are
dry. You have searched yourself and wondered why? BUT GOD
can heal your broken heart. With time and prayer God will
heal you from the inside straight through to the outside. He
will cover your mind with His blood. He will make you whole
again. He will restore what you have lost and give you double
for your trouble. He will bring back the desire to love and live
again. Oh yes! He can heal a broken heart. You are not a victim
but the victor. You will walk tall, hold your head up high and
Speak life over yourself daily. You will be the head, not the tail,
above, not beneath, you will be blessed above measure. Our
God is an awesome God. No matter your circumstance He is
the God of another chance. You will be able to walk in God's
grace, love and forgiveness. You will move on. You will keep
pressing forward. You will not only be a survivor but you will
thrive and be blessed abundantly in Jesus name. Trust God and
watch Him do it in your life! For His glory!!!

Prayer & Encouragement

Lord bless those who are going through divorce,
broken relationships or loss of a spouse. Let them know
that they are loved, they matter and they will survive.
They are more than conquerors. In Jesus name. Amen.

He Saves Families

Believe in the Lord Jesus Christ and you will be saved,
you and your household.
– Acts 16:31

God's mission has always been to save an entire family once a member has accepted Him. In Genesis He saved Noah, his wife and three sons, Shem, Ham and Japhet and all their wives (Gen. 7:1). When God got ready to destroy Sodom and Gomorrah He saved Lot and his family (Genesis 19:12). If you are a Christian today, you certainly care about your family members who are not yet saved. Stay in prayer for them because God's will is for all to come to eternal life. Families are very important to God. When He wanted to build a chosen nation, He started with a family. He took Abram and Sarai from among a clan of idol worshippers and brought them to Canaan where He blessed them and started a family through the miraculous birth of their son Isaac. The family blessing continued with Isaac marrying Rebecca and bringing forth the twins Esau and Jacob. Jacob being the chosen of the two brothers, was used by God to bring twelve sons who became the twelve tribes of God's chosen nation, Israel. From this nation the messiah was introduced to the world, Jesus Christ, our wonderful Savior, Lord and only begotten Son of God who left His home in glory to tabernacle with men and reconcile mankind to Our Father God. The family is important to God. Husbands, Wives, Fathers Mothers and children are all precious in His sight. God saves families.

Prayer & Encouragement

Lord help us to keep the sanctity of marriage (one man to one woman) so the true concept of family may be preserved. Amen.

When you're ready for marriage and a family, find a member of the opposite sex, get married and have children together. God honors proper marriage. (Hebrews 13:4). God saves families.

Children! What a Blessing!

Children are a gift from the LORD;
they are a reward from him.
– Psalm 127:3

I remember the days when we had many children in the house. There was always excitement. We stayed busy and there was always a friend or cousin to take on family trips.

Today our older children are grown, most with children of their own. My husband always says how much he misses the atmosphere of having a big family. BUT GOD completed our family with our youngest son seven years ago. Our little miracle baby. So we are not empty nesters yet.

The Lord has continued to fill our home with love, laughter and excitement thru this little boy with big beautiful brown eyes and a gigantic smile. Most weeks you can find us sitting at the computer looking at new pictures of the grandchildren. Thank God for the smiles and joy they bring us as well.

Prayer & Encouragement

Lord, bless Parents everywhere. Teach us Lord to share and show love to our children. Help them to appreciate the love that we share. In Jesus name. Amen.

The time and love you spend on a child is never wasted.

These Little Ones

And whoever gives one of these little ones only a
cup of cold water in the name of a disciple, assuredly,
I say to you, he shall by no means lose his reward.
– Matthew 10:42

Little ones here refers to the disciples and it extends today to all
God's children. Jesus said in another scripture if anyone should
hurt one of His children it would have been better for that
person who hurts that child or caused that child to sin to have
a millstone hung around his/her neck and that person drowned
in the deepest part of the sea (Matthew. 18:6).

A songwriter says, "Jesus loves the little children.
All the children of the world. Red, yellow,
black and white, all are precious in His sight.
Jesus loves the little children of the world."

Next time an opportunity arises to show kindness to a "child"
old or young, do not hesitate as you may be doing a good deed
to an angel (Hebrews 13:2).

Prayer and Encouragement

Lord help us to be kind and loving to
each child in this world. In Jesus name. Amen.
Each time the opportunity arises,
jump to it and extend some kindness to a "child."

The Steps of Good Men

The steps of a good man are ordered by the LORD,
and He delights in his way. Though he fall, he shall not be utterly
cast down; for the LORD upholds him with His hand.
– Psalm 37:23-24

This verse of scripture is fitting for all the leaders of this great country...
George Washington: 1789-1797; John Adams: 1797-1801;
Thomas Jefferson: 1801-1809; James Madison: 1809-1817; James Monroe 1817-1825; John Quincy Adams: 1825-1829; Andrew Jackson: 1829-1837;
Martin Van Buren: 1837-1841; William Henry Harrison: 1841; John Tyler: 1841-1845; James Knox Polk: 1845-1849; Zachary Taylor:1849-1850; Millard Fillmore: 1850-1853; Franklin Pierce: 1853-1857; James Buchanan: 1857-1861; Abraham Lincoln: 1861-1865; Andrew Johnson: 1865-1869; Ulysses Simpson Grant: 1869-1877; Rutherford Birchard Hayes: 1877-1881; James Abram Garfield: 1881; Chester Alan Arthur: 1881-1885; Grover Cleveland: 1885-1889, 1893-1897; Benjamin Harrison:1889-1893; William McKinley:1897-1901; Theodore Roosevelt: 1901-1909; William Howard Taft: 1909-1913; Woodrow Wilson:1913-1921; Warren Gamaliel Harding: 1921-1923; Calvin Coolidge:1923-1929; Herbert Clarke Hoover: 1929-1933; Franklin Delanor Roosevelt: 1933-1945; Harry S. Truman: 1945-1953: Dwight David Eisenhower: 1953-1961; John Fitzgerald Kennedy: 1961-1963; Lyndon Baines Johnson: 1963-1969; Richard Milhouse Nixon:1969-1974; Gerald Rudolph Ford: 1974-1977; James Earl Carter Jr. 1977-1981; Ronald Wilson Reagan: 1981-1989; George Herbert Walker Bush: 1989-1993; William Jefferson Clinton: 1993-2001; George Walker Bush: 2001-2009; Barrack Hussein Obama: 2009-present.

These men reached their heights not through sudden flight. But they, while their companions slept, were toiling upward through the night. God directed their steps and if you allow Him, He will direct yours too.

Prayer and Encouragement

Lord show us how to yield to Your will totally.
We pray in Jesus' mighty name. Amen.
God's will, His gifts and His talents are most times brought out when we go through tough experiences. Be sensitive to opportunities when they present themselves.

Thank God for Praying Mothers

Then (Hannah) made a vow and said,
"Oh Lord of hosts, if you will indeed look on the affliction
of your maidservant and remember me, and not forget your
maidservant, but will give your maidservant a male child,
then I will give him to the Lord all the days of his life,
and no razor shall come upon his head."
– 1 Samuel 1:11

There are millions of children in the world today who are involved in some affliction of sorts. Most of which have no adult relative caring for them. They are all left to the mercy of this world. A woman who has children in her care, whether biological or maternal, knows what it feels like for a child to not have anyone to turn to for care, love and protection. This is why an appeal is going out to women all over the world to care for at least one child who is not a part of her family and needs a motherly love, care and protection. It is well known that not every women can take on such responsibilities but at least praying for these children will untie God's hands so He can do something to help.

Remember God gave us dominion here and if we do not ask He is not at liberty to intervene in situations here. This is an appeal to women, especially women with a motherly instinct. Come together in prayer today for the children. Be a "Rachel" today and cry out for the children, refuse to be comforted for the children's sake. -Jerimiah 31:15; Mathew.2:18.

Prayer & Encouragement

Father we join mothers all over the world in asking
you to please intervene in children's lives today.
Send someone to defend, help and love these children.
Don't let these children hurt anymore we pray in Jesus' name.

Whatever you are able to do to help a child,
please do not hesitate to do so.
Please show unconditional love to
a child today. Be a "mother."

A Good Name

A good name is to be chosen rather than great riches.
– Proverbs 22:1a

There have been some great men to walk this earth and their contribution to their generation has impacted this world for years into the future. These men just didn't arrive overnight. It took time to prepare them for the major event that changed their lives forever. David fought a lion and a bear over time before having the courage to face goliath. Great leaders only found out they were great when they faced major obstacles and realize they had what it took to overcome these obstacles mostly because they had overcome other obstacles in their past. The major ones brought out the courage, tenacity, patience and the perseverance among other qualities developed in them over time. After the successful outcome came the good name that is to be chosen rather than great riches. Names that have paved the road in history and will be with us forever. When you are faced with great challenges see them as opportunities to pave the way to a great name and examples for others to learn by.

Prayer and Encouragement

Father help us to look to Jesus the greatest to walk this earth, whenever we face challenges that seem too enormous for us to face alone. Let us keep in mind that Jesus is always with us helping us. Amen. There is no temptation that has overtaken you but such as is common to man; God is faithful, who will not allow you to be tempted beyond what you are able, but with the temptation He will make a way of escape that you may be able to bear it. -1 Corinthians 10:13.

The Beginning Stage
of Leadership

Jesus said, "Do business till I come."
– Luke19:13

The first person a leader should
learn to lead is himself.
The first and best victory
is to conquer self.
– Plato

To be the best leader/servant you can be, first gain self-discipline. The Holy Spirit is with us to make us aware of "kingdom moments of opportunities" -situations in which we can "do business" in Jesus' name.

Prayer & Encouragement
Thank you Lord for the way to teach us
to be leaders in your kingdom.

Follow the Lord's leading so others may follow you.

Humble Yourself and He will Exalt You

God has chosen the foolish things of the world to confound the wise; and God has chosen the weak things of the world to confound the things which are mighty.
– 1 Corinthians. 1:27

God has a moment when he brings one of His children down real low before the other children, and then, suddenly, transport that child to a higher level in Him. It's His way of setting that child up without the child knowing.

We all should try to understand
what is happening in our lives
when unusual events are unfolding
and seek to learn what God is
attempting to teach or reveal to us.
Look for the positive.

God says in his Word in Hebrews chapter 12, our earthly fathers chasten us for their own pleasure But He (God) chastens us for our own profit, that we might be partakers of His holiness. Need anything more be said? When next time your hear the devil using someone to throw everything at you except the kitchen sink, calling you everything but the child of God, whom God called you, don't let it bother you. That is why God called and chose you. He chose the foolish of this world so He could confound the wise. He chose the base in this world to confound those who are mighty in their own eyes.

Remember what God has for
you no one can take it away.

Your time is coming and this could just be your season coming up. Remember what was mentioned at the beginning of today's devotion. It's a setup from God.

Whatever God has in store for you be wise to receive it at the appointed time however which way it comes.

Prayer & Encouragement

Lord help us not to miss our moment by reading the message the enemy tries to put in our thought process when we're being set up for a promotion from You. Amen.

Just as we should see success as failure turned inside out, let us see God's message as what He is working on in our lives. Get the correct message and respond correctly regardless of how it seems to be delivered from God. Thank God for revelation knowledge which defeats the plan of the enemy and step into your season

It's A New Day, A New Season

I will bless the LORD at all times; His praise
shall continually be in my mouth.
– Psalm 34:1

This is the day the Lord has made. We will rejoice and be glad in it. Lord, consecrate us to the work You have planned for us just in this day, and consecrate this day unto the Holy Service you have planned for Your kingdom. This day is a day we've never seen before and will never see again. Help us to fulfill Your will and Your purpose for us today. We want to make the most of this day our Lord as time wasted can never be regained. Let us make hay together while the sun shines. You are love, You are life, You are Lord over everything. Alpha, Omega, Jehovah, our King of Kings. Lord You are our wonderful way maker, You are worthy of our offering, hallowed be Your name. We present ourselves to You Lord this morning, living sacrifice, holy, acceptable; for this is our reasonable form of worship which we were created by You to do. Amen!!!

Prayer and Encouragement

Lord we praise You for who You are today.
We worship You in this new season.
We're not going to let anyone or
anything stop us from praising God.

It's the Lord's Day

Thank You Father for a brand new day.

Bless us individually and collectively as we congregate to minister to You, the audience of one, on this Your day. Prepare our hearts to receive the spiritual food You will deliver to us today through Your anointed vessel, the one who will stand in John's shoes.

Refresh Your anointing power upon us all
and let it be all of You and none of us as
You hide us behind the cross today.

Father again we are coming before You in the name of Jesus. Lord we're coming to present everyone who will be used by you this morning in services globally. Especially those who have made request here on the various social networks. Bless them and anoint them from on high we pray. Use them for Your glory to minister to your flock today. In the mighty name of Jesus we pray, amen!!!

Prayer and Encouragement

Thank You Father for your Holy Spirit.
Go forth and allow the Lord to use you.

Fourth of July

I am the Lord your God, Who brought you out of
the land of Egypt, out of the house of bondage.
– Exodus 20:2

Like Israel God has helped many countries gain independence over centuries now and America is one such country which gained independence in 1776. Ever since, this great nation has been employing its citizens in the armed forces of America to guard its borders and since the 19th century has been sending troops abroad to protect its interest and properties. There is a greater freedom or independence that has been about from A.D. 33 and that is everyone on this earth having the choice to accept freedom from the bondage and oppression of sin. Jesus opened the door for mankind to be free or independent of Satan and his lifestyle of opposing God or rebelling against Him. Jesus conquered satan at Calvary on that faithful day and took back the keys to the kingdom as well as the keys to death, hell and the grave and everything else that was stolen from us including dominion on earth which were stolen from us when Satan (in the form of a serpent) tricked Adam into obeying him (by using Eve) and rebelling against God. As we celebrate the fourth of July, let us not forget that our heavenly Father also gave us independence from the enemy of darkness too. Praise God!!!

Prayer and Encouragement

Father as we celebrate independence the fourth of July help
us to keep in mind that You gave us life and You gave it
abundantly. Amen. We should celebrate our independence.
Both physically (July 4th) and spiritually (being born again).

Another Thanksgiving

In everything give thanks; for this is the
will of God in Christ Jesus for you.
– 1 Thessalonians 5:18

In everything we should give thanks and on this day of thanksgiving everyone in this country is thankful for another year of prosperity.

Overall this country in spite of hardships
and the economy outlook has been
successful thanks to the glory of God.

Let us now look forward to a new year with new expectations and the challenges we are ready to face and overcome in the mighty name of Jesus our help. God bless everyone.

Prayer and Encouragement

Father we once more Thank You for another year and all it entails. Thank You for being our provider, our way maker, our deliverer, our healer. Thank You for Your peace, Your joy and Thank You Lord for Your strength.
In Jesus name we pray. Amen.
We should give thanks to our
God every opportunity we get.

After Thanksgiving

The turkey and the helpings are almost gone. All the family members and other guests have left on their journey back to their point of origin. Everyone gave thanks and are very happy to have been in attendance. All participated in the clean-up and now you're alone together once again. Everyone is grown and have their own family and will be looking forward to do it all over again next year.

It was a beautiful time together. Some families had three or four generations sharing together. Others had up to five or more generations.

God is good and worthy to be praised. Oh give thanks unto our Lord for He is good and is mercy endures forever.

It is truly through his abundant blessings and his tender loving kindness or mercy that all that gathered this thanksgiving holiday was able to do so. Yes, in all the wining, dining and the reveling, do not forget who made all this possible and keep a thankful heart, even after Thanksgiving!

Thank You God!!!

Prayer and Encouragement

Father thank you again, and again and again..
Give thanks with a grateful heart.

Blessings

Today is the day the Lord has made, we will rejoice and be glad in it. Every good and perfect gift is from God. God gave this day a gift to us and we dedicate this day to God. Every plan and purpose of God for us in this day is fulfilled. We receive every blessing in store for us today from our Father God. We are blessed, we are blessed, we are blessed, we are blessed in the city, we're blessed in the field. We're blessed when we come and when we go. We cast down every stronghold. Sickness and poverty must cease. The devil is defeated in the name of Jesus Christ today. Jesus has conquered Satan and made us victorious. We have the keys to the kingdom. Whatever we bind on earth is already bound in heaven. Whatever we loose on earth is already loosed in heaven. We have power over the power of the enemy. We have the power to walk on serpents and scorpions. The devil is under our feet. We are His. He calls us by His name. We are Christians and nothing shall by any means hurt us. Because we believe in You and have been baptized, we are saved. In Your name we cast out devils, we speak with new tongues, We take up serpents and drink deadly things which cannot harm us. We lay hands on the sick and they recover. We are blessed!

Prayer and Encouragement

Father thank You for your many blessings. Amen!
Take comfort. The greatest gift and blessing is
to know that your name is written in the book of life.

I Remember

The Comforter which is the Holy Ghost, whom the Father will
send in my name, He shall teach you all things, and bring all
things to your remembrance, whatsoever I've said unto you.
– John 14:26

A title such as "I REMEMBER" reminds one so much of the
poem, "I Wonder" by Jeannie Kirby. I remember how I wondered
when I recited that poem. I wonder why the grass is green and
why the wind is never seen. Who taught the birds to build a
nest and told the trees to take a rest. Who hang those clouds so
high... Yes that one baffled me as a child and as a youth. Until I
found the reason the wind is never seen. You see the metaphor,
or is it the personification one may draw from John 3:8, can
only be discerned when the Holy Spirit reveals Himself in the
meaning or explanation of that passage. That which is born of
th flesh is flesh and that which is born of the Spirit is Spirit.
After all, the flesh is at enmity with the Spirit and the Spirit is
at enmity with the flesh. One cannot serve two masters at once
and therefore needs the Holy Spirit to breakdown the meaning
of scripture. The Word of God is foolishness to the natural man
as it is spiritually discerned.

Jesus is the one who gives us His Spirit (the Spirit of Christ is
the Holy Spirit) and without Him (The Holy Spirit) we cannot
make it in this world. Let me explain this statement before I get
my head chewed off by those who misunderstand. When one
repents of his/her sins and ask forgiveness, he/she invites Jesus
in his/her heart and immediately the Holy Spirit comes and
dwells inside that person. Without this happening one cannot
"make it" or enter the Kingdom of God. There is a further step
which is not a requirement to enter heaven but is a far easier
way to live this life to its fullest and achieve all that God has for

you here and in eternity future and how does one get all this, by being "baptized" in the Holy Spirit or being "filled" with the Holy Spirit (not a requirement to "make it" but very important to make living the Christian life easier). The Holy Spirit teaches us all things we require to be strong, wise, mature and whole Christians. He reveals all truths to us. The Holy Spirit brings everything to our remembrance and He rebukes and convicts. Without Him it is almost impossible or totally impossible as some would agree, to be successful in living this Christian life. If you see yourself being here for any lengthy period of time living for God, I suggest, NO, I implore you, get the baptism of the Holy Spirit.

You'll be glad you did when you see how
much easier it is to live this life with Him.

He walks beside you, He is inside you, His presence surrounds you and he guides you every step of the way. Now, can you refuse or deny someone like that, access to your whole life?

Prayer and Encouragement

Lord, like the woman at the well who begged You to
give her "this water" so she would never thirst again we ask
You please give us your Spirit, The Holy Spirit so we will not
fail to hit the mark. In Jesus name. Amen. If you don't have
the Holy Spirit as yet, pray to be filled with Him.
It's the _BEST_ thing that could ever happen
to anyone in their lifetime.

How to Please
Our Heavenly Father

For without faith it is impossible to please God.
For him that comes to God must believe that He is and
that He is a rewarder of those who diligently seek Him.
– Hebrews 11:6

Our Bible tells us in John 4:24 that God our Father is a Spirit
and we who worship Him must worship Him in spirit and in
truth. We must worship our God in spirit because He is Spirit
and we are spirits having souls and living in bodies. We must
see Him for Who He truly is. Therefore we must worship Him
in truth. How best may we do that but seeing our God through
spiritual eyes or through faith. We cannot please our heavenly
Father without faith for whoever comes to God our father must
believe that He exists and that He rewards those who seek, and
seek, and seek Him. Seek the Lord while He may be found, call
upon Him while He is near (Isaiah 55:6). How do we do all this
seeking of someone we cannot see with our natural eyes? How
do we believe that He is? Simple, we walk by faith and not by
sight (2 Corinthians 5:7). We look through spiritual eyes and
see the invisible (2 Kings 6:17) and if we can see the invisible
we can do the impossible.

Prayer & Encouragement

Lord help us to realize any obstacle we face in life we can
overcome by having faith in You the Omnipotent God. Have
faith in God. He is bigger than any problem, question or fear.
He will see you through.

The Vision

Where there is no vision the people perish.
– Proverbs 29:18

Everyone on this earth should have a unique vision for himself or herself and if you belong to some group or organization, share in the common vision of that group or organization. Your unique vision may be the goals you set for yourself, be it long term or short term. And then you may share in the common goals of your family and, on your job with your coworkers and finally, your church. In order of importance the five most important persons or things in your life should be prioritized in this way. First should be God. Second to God is your spouse. Then family, then your job and finally church work. This shows where we should channel our energy most in fulfilling our purpose here on earth. Without a vision we will perish. An old proverb says, "He who does not know where he is going will probably end up some place else." Know the vision of whatever organization you are a part of and know your role in executing that vision. Seek revelation from God regarding your personal vision and seek direction from Him in fulfilling it. Then you will know why on earth you are you here and live your life with purpose.

Prayer & Encouragement

Father please help us to do our part to fulfill the purpose
for which you created us. Lord, help us to have clear vision.
Help us to write the vision and make it plain so others can run
with it. Amen. Stick with God. You can never go wrong.

Respect the Messenger

Most assuredly, I say to you, he who receives whomsoever
I send receives me; and he who receives me
receives Him who sent me.
– John 13:20

Beautiful words are these coming straight from the Savior's mouth. If I can receive from a famous pastor or evangelist I should receive from everyone else who brings a message from the Lord. Therefore if a Pastor is ministering I must receive from our God through His anointed servant, what thus saith the Lord. If you find you're not comfortable receiving from any of God servants then you're disrespecting and dishonoring God, the one who sent His messenger with His message to bless you and you will block and miss out on important blessings. Remember God is no respecter of persons and He sees everyone equally before His eyes. He created everyone and none is righteous, no not one. We are only righteous because God our father sees Jesus when He looks at us and we're the righteousness of God in Christ Jesus. If God were to look on everyone in this world the way some look and judge others, there would not be one soul left on this earth for all have sin and come short of the glory of God (Romans. 3:23). Just as He looks beyond all faults and sees our need for a Savior so we should see ourselves and not consider ourselves qualified to judge anyone. Judge not, less ye be judged (Matthew 7:1). Accept and respect the messenger from God and see him/her as you see God. Whoever accepts the messenger accepts and respects Him who sent the messenger.

Prayer & Encouragement

Father help us to humble ourselves and esteem
our brothers and sisters from every background
that you send to minister to us. Amen.

Accept, respect, honor and bless
the man or woman of God at all times.
By doing so, you certainly will not block your blessings.

Assemble Yourselves for Worship

Do not forsake the assembling of yourselves together, as is
the manner of some, but exhort one another, and much
the more as you see the day approaching.
– Hebrews 10:25

Christians in the world assembly on Sunday's to remember the resurrection of the Lord. There is an even greater importance to man for celebrating Jesus' resurrection by assembling ourselves on this day. The great benefit to each of us from doing this is the blessings we each receive from the Lord. We should exhort each other as we see the day of the Lord approaching. God blesses His people when they come together and do everything to Him and for Him. He is the sole audience whenever we assemble ourselves for worship. As we do everything as unto Him on that day He shows his appreciation for our worship by sending down the blessings upon us. It doesn't matter the assembly size. Whether two, two hundred, two thousand or twenty thousand, numbers do not matter to God. He is the center of the worship and He in any service is "the majority." Don't forsake the assembling of yourselves whenever the opportunity is there. And always be aware that the important thing is, where we assemble in His name, He will always be there. Matthew 18:20.

Prayer & Encouragement

Father help us to never forsake the assembling of
ourselves together knowing You will be there to bless us.
If you have to be absent from the assembly, don't stay away
for too long as some have strayed too far and
stayed too long and never came back.

The Lord's Supper

Jesus took bread, blessed and broke it, and gave it to
the disciples and said, "Take, eat, this is my body.
– Matthew 26:26

On the night Jesus was betrayed He took bread and blessed and broke it, and gave it to the disciples and told them to take and eat it for this is His body which is broken for all. Then He took the cup and gave thanks and gave it to the disciples and told them to drink all of it for this is His blood of the new covenant which is shed for the remission of the sins of everyone. On that night The Lord's Supper was instituted with the promise that whenever we, Jews and Gentile alike partake we do show the Lord's death until He returns. It was the end of annual commemoration and celebration of the Passover where only Jews and sojourners with the Jews could partake. Our Jesus it was believed by the Jewish Nation had come to Rescue Israel from the Roman rule and restore the nation to dominance. However the deliverance went much farther than the Nation of Israel. It was the whole world including Israel that He came to deliver not just from Roman rule but from the clutches of Satan and the bondage and penalty of sin. Jesus, the deliverer of the whole world has instituted a way we can stay connected to Him, remain alive in Him and grow in Him.

Prayer and Encouragement

Lord let us keep on taking Your communion so we will
remain in You. Stay connected to God, eat of His flesh
and drink of His blood of the new covenant knowing
as often as you do this you do show His death until
He returns and you're taking life.

Such Blessing Our Storehouses Cannot Contain

"Bring all the tithe into the storehouse, that there may be food in
My house, and try me now in this," Says the Lord of hosts, "If I
will not open for you the windows of heaven and pour out for you
such blessing, that there will not be room enough to receive it."
– Malachai.3:10

"Prove me!" Great words to hear from a friend. When these words come from God be sure to know that of a surety what he's telling you to prove Him in will be done. In the book of Numbers He says, "I am not a man that I should lie" -Num. 23:19. He also says His word shall not go out and come back to Him void but will accomplish whatever He sends it forth to accomplish -Isaiah 55:11. Now our God says bring all the tithe into the storehouse. Not some, or what you can for whatever reason. All the tithe. God is a loving God. He will not withhold blessings when we have done what is requested or expected in order for us to receive. He will do what He says. No need to use what you're expected to give and block your blessing. What blessing? I hear someone asked. I've been asking for a car for years now. Someone else says they've been waiting for a house. Well the blessing is not only those things. Are your children getting good grades in school and behaving themselves at home and abroad? Is your marriage intact? Are you able to afford all the bills and provide food for your family? All these and a lot more are blessings from the Lord. And even if you are short in these areas just the fact that you're living is a blessing. Bring all the tithes into His storehouse and you will be sure to receive your fair share of blessings from heaven's open window that your barns and storehouses will not be able to contain it.

Prayer & Encouragement

Lord, help us to obey your every command to us so our blessings will continuously flow to us from heaven. Amen.

Trust God. His Words are true and sure.

We Are All One

For as the body is one and has many members,
but all the members of that one body, being many,
are one body, so also is Christ.
– 1 Corinthians 12:12

God's work is so amazing. His ministry is past finding out. He has placed every child of His, every believer into the body of His son, Jesus Christ. The Church is the body of Christ. Everyone is a member of Christ body and should find out the part of the body he/she is and consequently his/her function in the body.

Prayer & Encouragement

Father help us to find our place in you and do our best at what you have for us to do. Lord help us to realize that we each have different gifts, abilities, talents and assignments but they are all to work together for the glory of God. It's all about You Lord. Your work, Your plan, Your mission, Your love…. Help us to be united as One Body in Christ. No division. No schism. Just One Body. Amen

Lord help us to ask – "Lord, what would You have me to do?" You are unique. There's only one you. Every page in your destiny was written before you entered this world through your mother's birth canal. Nothing can stop you from fulfilling your destiny but you.

Change the Atmosphere

Assuredly, I say to you, wherever this gospel is
preached in the whole world, what this woman has
done will also be told as a memorial to her.
– Matthew 26:13

The story in the Bible of the woman with the alabaster box is well known to many around the world.

During Passion Week she enters a room while Jesus is visiting with one called Simon the leper and opens an alabaster flask with costly fragrant oil and poured it on His head as he sat at a table. The fragrance from this costly ointment fill the room to everyone's amazement. The aroma was so sweet and so strong that Jesus' disciples could readily tell the value and how many poor people the proceeds from the sale of such an ointment would have cared for.

Jesus had to remind them the value of the act rather than the value of the ointment and the fact that the poor will always be around but He, the one who cares for the poor the most in the world, would not always be in the flesh and present with them.

The very act of this woman changed the atmosphere that moment and so should we. Whenever we enter anywhere the moment we spring into action or even before we do, others present there should take note that we have been with Jesus or that we're Jesus followers.

Prayer and Encouragement

Lord we want to change the atmosphere wherever we go.
May we acknowledge your presence at all times.
Work in and us and through us in Jesus name we pray. Amen.

You are chosen to change the atmosphere. Go on your
journey in the name of Jesus. Be obedient and don't be afraid.

It Surely Is a Good Friday

He was wounded for our transgression,
bruised for our iniquity, the chastisement for our peace
was upon Him, and by His stripes we are healed.
– Isaiah 53:5

Jesus suffered for a long, long time before being placed on the cross. Then on the cross He bore so much pain in addition to taking on the sins of the whole world. Past, present and future. How could one man bear so much? Because He was one hundred percent God and one hundred percent man. That's how. Had He not been perfect, He could not have paid the price for the sins of all mankind. God did not spare His only begotten Son. He knew how much it would hurt Him to see His only Son die a death He did not deserve. But when He saw mankind whom He loves just as much and knew we were like sheep for slaughter, not knowing what we were doing or where we were heading, He had to do something to save us. Yes, that Friday was a Good Friday to die. Today, we celebrate that Friday, it is a Good Friday to celebrate a man's death that made us have abundant and eternal life. It was a good day to give life to billions. It was expedient for one to die for nations to live. Who else could do this? Only the Lamb slain from before the foundation of the earth. The Alpha and Omega, The Beginning and the End, the First and the Last, He who was and is and is to come, He who was alive then dead and is alive again forevermore. He alone has been found worthy.

Prayer and Encouragement

Lord thank You for the finished work on that day.
It was a Good Friday for those billions who accepted.
Be of good cheer. It's A Good Friday.

His Body Was in the Tomb All Day Saturday

(Pilate), command that the tomb be made secure until the
third day, lest His disciples come by night and steal Him away,
and say to the people, "He has risen from the dead."
So the last deception will be worse than the first.
– Matthew 27:64

He had suffered hard and long. He hung His head and died. He was taken down from the cross, wrapped in cloth and placed in a borrowed tomb. He was there all night Friday night all day Saturday, all night Saturday night, but early Sunday morning, He Rose from the dead!!! No grave could hold His body down. The events that took place in that grave on Saturday was that the body laid there guarded by two Cherubim, one at His head and one at His feet. They were there from the moment the stone was rolled into place at the mouth of the tomb until Jesus rose early that first Easter Morning. The High priest and the scribes went to Pilate and requested that the tomb be secure so they could ensure that His body remains in the tomb but little did they know that nothing could prevent the body of Jesus from the resurrection power of the Holy Ghost. And that power is in everyone who is a born again believer in Jesus Christ. Yes the body was there all day Saturday while His Spirit was busy setting captives free from hades. Early Sunday morning He rose. Glory to God!!!

Prayer and Encouragement

Lord let us never forget that You are alive forevermore.
Go tell it on the mountain, over the hills and everywhere that
Jesus Christ is alive and well forevermore.

He Is Risen!!!

(The Angel) said to them (Mary, the mother of Jesus,
Mary Magdalene, and Salome), "Do not be alarmed.
You seek Jesus of Nazareth, who was crucified. He is risen!
He is not here. See the place where they had laid Him.
– Mark 16:6

The women went in search of a dead Jesus. People are still looking for a dead Jesus today who they think can do nothing. They wander about daily going through life as though nothing matters. Everything is just as it is. Nothing changes. These people consider life as though they cannot make things happen. They just watch as things happen to them. Jesus is no longer in the grave and we can do all things through Him who strengthens us. Turn to the living Savior today and let Him change things in your life from just mundane to supernatural. He can do it and He will if you let Him. There is nothing too hard for God. His hands are not too short that He is not able. He can do all things. His word to us is, "nothing in this world is too difficult for me. With men some things are impossible but not so with me (God), for with me all things are possible." Don't go looking for a dead Jesus. He is risen!! He is alive!!

Prayer and Encouragement

Father help us to present Jesus to the world
as our Savior, alive forevermore. Amen.
Because Jesus is risen you can face all your troubles,
because He is alive you can face all your fears.
With Him all things are possible, only believe.
Praise God!!!

After The Resurrection

He rose on the third day according to the scriptures, He was
seen by Cephas then by the twelve. After that He was seen
by five hundred brethren at once, of whom the greater part
remain to the present, but some have fallen asleep.
– 1 Corinthians 15:4-6

When Jesus arose He revealed Himself to His followers only,
during a forty day period and then gave them a commission just
before ascending into Heaven. He walked this earth for forty
days after His resurrection doing good and revealing scripture
fulfillment wherever He went. After revealing Himself to Mary
Magdalene, out of whom He had cast out seven devils, He
revealed Himself to the disciples, Peter being the first, then to
five hundred followers including His mother and all the other
women who accompanied them on their journeys during His
ministry. James His brother later saw Him and then all the
apostles. Jesus spoke with His disciples revealing to them that
John baptized with water but we all would be baptized with the
Holy Spirit.

Then when they asked if He would restore the kingdom to Israel
He answered, "It is not for you to know times or seasons which
the Father has put in His own authority. But you shall receive
power when the Holy Spirit has come upon you; and you shall
be witnesses to me in Jerusalem, and in all Judea and Samaria,
and to the end of the earth. Acts 1:6-8. Then while speaking
and giving His commission for us to go into all the world and
make disciples of all nations, baptizing them in the name of
the Father and of the Son and of the Holy Spirit. Then to teach
these nations to observe all things that He commanded and lo
He is with us always, even to the end of the age, He was taken
up in a cloud.

Prayer and Encouragement

Father thank you for the record in Your written word which proves that Jesus arose and is alive forevermore. Amen. Because He lives we can face tomorrow.

Oh What A Day That Will Be

And God will wipe away every tear from their eyes; there shall
be no more death, nor sorrow, nor crying. There shall
be no more pain, for the former things have passed away.
– Revelation. 21:4

Oh what a glory that day will be. When all the Saints go
marching in. Oh what a hallelujah grand day. What a glorious
day that will be. Oh what a day that will be, when my Jesus I
shall see. When I look upon His face, the one who saved me by
His grace. Oh when He takes me by the hand, and leads me to
the Promised Land. Oh what a day, a glorious day, that will be.
John the revelator said he saw a new heaven and a new earth for
the first heaven and the old earth had passed away. Then he saw
the holy city, New Jerusalem, coming down out of heaven from
God. Then he heard a loud voice from heaven saying, "Behold
the tabernacle of God is with men, and He shall dwell with them
and they shall be His people. God Himself shall be with them
and be their God. And God will wipe away every tear from
their eyes; there shall be no more death nor sorrow nor crying.
There shall be no more pain, for the former things have passed
away." Then He who sat on the throne said, "Behold I make all
things new." Hallelujah!!! Praise the Lord!!! I look forward to
that day with great anticipation and comfort myself right now
with these thoughts. Thank You Jesus!!!

Prayer & Encouragement

Lord we can't wait for that glorious day which begins the longest period of our existence, eternity. Help us never to lose focus of You sand your perfect will for us. Amen.

Don't You want to hear Him say- "Well Done". Amen. Comfort yourselves with the thoughts God commanded.

Be Ready When He Comes

Then Martha, as soon as she heard that Jesus
was coming, went and met Him.
– John 11:20

When Jesus shows up we need to be ready. If we were told to expect a visit from a high profiled politician like a senator, a congressman, a mayor, the governor of the state you live in, or even the president you would see to it that everywhere in the home is properly cleaned and in order. Well when a more honorable than any other man on this earth comes to visit He only require that we be ready in spirit. Be ready when He comes. Jesus the Son of God is omnipresent and being everywhere at the same time, seeing and knowing everything, past, present and future and then having all power over every other power in the entire universe, there is nothing that escapes Him or surprises Him at any time.

There is no need to jump to get everything in order in the home or neighborhood because He is coming. He is already there. All He requires is that we give Him our hearts just as we are. That is the readiness He requires. Let's look at some examples of what happens when He showed up during His time here on earth when He gave up His glory for a time and minimize His omnipresence ability indicated in the Gospels of the New Testament.

In Matthew 8:1-3 a leper came up to Him and worshipped Him, asking if He was willing He could heal him. Jesus had just come down from a mountain and walked in that very direction where the leper was and that leper was ready, so Jesus answered him "I am willing, be thou clean." And immediately his leprosy was cleansed. In verses 5-13 of the same chapter Jesus entered

Capernaum and a centurion was ready for Him. He asked Jesus to heal his servant and when Jesus offered to come to his house to heal the servant the centurion gave such a startling explanation of why Jesus could do it from where he was that Jesus commended him above any Jew and the servant was healed that self-same hour.

In verses 14-15, Jesus showed up at Peter's house where his mother-in-law was sick with a fever, as soon as Jesus touched her the fever left her and she got up and ministered to everyone present.

In verses 16-17 everyone was informed throughout the neighborhood that Jesus was visiting and they brought to Him many possessed with devils and many that were sick and the Word of God says Jesus cast out the devils and healed everyone.

Then Jesus shows up on the other side of the Sea of Galilee in verses 28-32 and casts a vast number of demons who called themselves "legion" out of two possessed with them, into some swine and the swine ran down a steep slope into the sea and drowned themselves. When Jesus shows up BE READY for He means business.

In John 11 Jesus came to Bethany with a plan. He showed up four days after a friend died after being urged to come and heal him of a sickness which was sure to take his life days earlier. Jesus certainly had a plan. He prayed at the graveside, "Father, I thank thee that thou hast heard me. And I knew that thou hear me always, but because of the people which stand by I said it, that they may believe that thou hast sent me." Jesus waited until Lazarus, His friend whom He loved very much (chapter 11:3) died and was buried for four days before showing up. Talk about not coming when He's needed or not on our time but on

His. He showed up that late to do a mightier work which would signify to the people present there and to the world for future generations that He is the Son of God and He is present in the flesh sent by God the Father to fulfill His purpose. Then he cried with a loud voice, "Lazarus! Come forth!"

Many preachers have said that had He not called Lazarus by name, everyone who had died from the first man Adam, all the way down to Lazarus and any that may have just died after Lazarus, up to that point, would have got up and "come forth." As soon as Jesus finished that command, he that was dead for four days and was wrapped in burial cloth and had a napkin tied around his face came hopping out of the grave in answer to his name. Everyone that was there was astonished at this amazing act. Be Ready When Jesus Comes!

Prayer and Encouragement

Father God in the name of Jesus. I don't want to live my life
and end up in hell. You said that You are coming back for
Your church without a spot or wrinkle. Cleanse me, wash me,
heal me, deliver me, set me free. Help me to live my
life in such a way that You will be glorified.

Help me Lord that when my time comes
I will be ready to meet You face to face.

Lord help us to be ready when You come and not miss
the hour of our visitation. Amen!!!

Pray always and watch, for you know
not the hour of your visitation. Are You ready???

Prayer to God
Psalm 63

O God, You are my God, Early will I seek You. My soul thirsts for You, my flesh longs for You, In a dry and thirsty land where there is no water. So I have looked for You in the sanctuary, to see Your power and Your glory. Because Your loving kindness is better than life, my lips shall praise You. Thus I will bless You while I live. I will lift up my hands in Your name. My soul shall be satisfied as with marrow and fatness. And my mouth shall be praised with joyful lips. When I remember You on my bed, I meditate on You in the night watches, because You have been my help. Therefore in the shadow of Your wings I will rejoice. My soul follows close behind You. Your right hand upholds me. But those who seek my life to destroy it, shall go into the lower parts of the earth. They shall fall by the sword. They shall be a portion for jackals. But the king shall rejoice in God. Everyone who swears by Him shall glory. But the mouth of those who speak lies shall be stopped.

Prayer and Encouragement

Lord in the midst of every challenge or obstacle sent
to distract Your people today, help us stay focused on You,
our great shield and our exceeding great reward. Amen.
Trials are here to make us not break us. Embrace them. If He
takes you to a trial, He'll see you through it. Anyone trying
to ensnare you is being used by the enemy. Have no fear,
Jesus is with you. He is fighting all your battles for you.
He promised never to leave you nor forsake you.

The Day of Pentecost
Acts Chapter 2

On the day of Pentecost all the Lord's followers were together in one place. Suddenly there was a noise from heaven like the sound of a mighty wind! It filled the house where they were meeting. Then they saw what looked like fiery tongues moving in all directions, and a tongue came and settled on each person there. The Holy Spirit took control of everyone and they began speaking whatever languages the Spirit let them speak. Many religious Jews from every country in the world were living in Jerusalem. And when they heard this noise a crowd gathered. But they were surprised because they were hearing everything in their own languages. They were excited and amazed and said, "Don't all these who are speaking come from Galilee? Then why do we hear them speaking our own languages? Some of us are from Parthia, Media, and Elam. Others are from Mesopotamia, Judea, Cappadocia, Pontus, Asia, Phrygia, Pamphylia, Egypt, parts of Lybia, near Cyrene, Rome, Crete and Arabia. Some of us were born Jews, and others of us have chosen to be Jews. Yet we all hear them using our own languages to tell the wonderful things God has done." Everyone was excited and confused. Some of them even kept asking each other, "What does all this mean?" Others made fun of the Lord's followers and said, "They are drunk." {Acts 2:1-13 (CEV)}. We have a great reason to celebrate the day of Pentecost as this was the day Jesus' church which He said He would build started. It's on the solid rock of Jesus Christ and the gates of hell has not and will never prevail against it. Glory to God!!!

Prayer & Encouragement

Father continue to reveal to us your church,
Your will for us and grant us the power and strength to
continue steadfast in Your purpose. Amen!

Remain steadfast, unmovable in the work for
which you were called, knowing that He who
began this good work in you will complete it

Our Father & Our Shepherd
Psalm 23

The Lord is my shepherd (to feed guide and shield me), I shall not lack. He makes me lie down in (fresh tender) green pastures; He leads me beside the still and restful waters. He refreshes and restores my life (myself): He leads me in the paths of righteousness (uprightness and right standing with Him -not for my earning it, but) for His name's sake. Yea, though I walk through the (deep sunless) valley of the shadow of death. I will fear or dread no evil, for You are with me: Your rod (to protect) and Your staff (to guide), they comfort me. You prepare a table before me in the presence of my enemies. You anoint my head with oil: my (brimming) cup runs over. Surely or only goodness, mercy, and unfailing love shall follow me all the days of my life, And through the length of my days the house of the Lord (and His presence) shall be my dwelling place.

Prayer & Encouragement

Thank You Lord for being a loving and caring Father. Thank You for your leading, guiding and protection. Lord thank You for looking out for me and taking time to care about me. Thank You for wrapping me in Your arms of love and protection. Thank You for making me feel secure, calm and at ease because I know You are watching over me. Amen.

He will take care of you.
None that is given to Him
by the Father will He lose.

A Broken and Contrite Heart He'll Not Despise
Psalm 51

Have mercy upon me, O God, according to Your steadfast love; according to the multitude of Your tender mercy and loving kindness blot out my transgressions. Wash me thoroughly (and repeatedly) from my iniquity and cleanse me, and make me wholly pure from my sin! For I am conscious of my transgressions and I acknowledge them; my sin is ever before me. Against You, You only have I sinned and done that which is evil in Your sight, so that You are justified in Your sentence and faultless in Your judgment. Behold, I was brought forth in (a state of) iniquity; my mother was sinful who conceived me (and I too am sinful). Behold You desire truth in the inner being; make me therefore to know wisdom in my inmost heart. Purify me with hissop, and I shall be clean (ceremonially); wash me and I shall (in reality) be whiter than snow. Make me to hear joy and gladness and be satisfied; let the bones which You have broken rejoice.

Hide Your face from my sins
and blot out all my guilt and iniquities.
Create in me a clean heart, O God,
and renew a right, persevering,
and steadfast spirit within me.

Cast me not away from Your presence and take not Your Holy Spirit from me. Restore to me the joy of Your salvation and uphold me with a willing spirit. Then will I teach transgressors your ways, and sinners shall be converted and turn to You. Deliver me from blood guiltiness and death, O God, the God of my Salvation, and my tongue shall sing aloud of Your righteousness

(Your rightness and Your justice). O Lord, open my lips, and my mouth shall show forth Your praise. For You delight not in sacrifice, or else would I give it; You find no pleasure in burnt offering. My sacrifice (the sacrifice acceptable) to God is a broken spirit; a broken and contrite heart (broken down with sorrow for sin and humbly and thoroughly penitent), such, O God You will not despise. Do good in Your good pleasure to Zion; rebuild the walls of Jerusalem. Then will You delight in the sacrifices of righteousness, justice, and right, with burnt offering and whole burnt offering; then bullocks will be offered upon Your alter.

Prayer & Encouragement

Thank You Lord for being the God Who is slow to chide and swift to bless. Thank You Lord for healing my broken and wounded spirit. Thank You Lord for picking me up when I fall. Thank You Lord for renewing me, refreshing me, restoring me and reviving me. Thank You for making me brand new. A new creature in Christ. Amen.

The Lord our God loves us so much.
He is ready with open arms to receive us
and forgive us when we falter.

Praise the Lord
Psalm 150

Praise the LORD.
Praise God in His sanctuary:
Praise Him in the firmament of His power.
Praise Him for His mighty acts:
Praise Him according
to His excellent greatness.
Praise Him with the sound of the trumpet:
Praise Him with the psaltery and harp.
Praise Him with the timbrel and dance:
Praise Him with stringed
instruments & organs.
Praise Him upon the loud cymbals:
Praise Him upon the
high sounding cymbals.
Let everything that hath breath
praise the LORD.
Praise Ye the LORD

Prayer & Encouragement

Lord, help me to praise and worship You with my
whole heart. Father I know that You delight in our
praise of You. I love to praise You Lord!!!
Yes, I love to praise Your holy name.

Our Father
Matthew 6:9-13

Our Father,
Who art in heaven,
Hallowed be thy name,
Thy kingdom come,
Thy will be done on earth
as it is in heaven.
Give us this day our daily bread,
Forgive us this day our trespasses
As we forgive those who
trespass against us.
Lead us not into temptation
But deliver us from evil.
For Thine is the kingdom
And the power
And the glory,
Forever, Amen!!!

Prayer & Encouragement

Lord, teach me how to pray.
Lord, I know You love it when we take time
to talk to You. Lord help me to take the time
to listen to You. Speak to my heart Lord.

The Lord, the Only Savior
Isaiah 45

Thus says the LORD:
"The labor of Egypt and merchandise of Cush
And of the Sabeans, men of stature,
Shall come over to you, and they shall be yours;
They shall walk behind you,
They shall come over in chains;
And they shall bow down to you.
They will make supplication to you, saying,
'Surely God is in you,
And there is no other;
There is no other God.'"
Truly You are God, who hide Yourself,
O God of Israel, the Savior!
They shall be ashamed
And also disgraced, all of them;
They shall go in confusion together,
Who are makers of idols.
But Israel shall be saved by the LORD
With an everlasting salvation;
You shall not be ashamed or disgraced
Forever and ever.

For thus says the LORD,
Who created the heavens,
Who is God,
Who formed the earth and made it,
Who has established it,
Who did not create it in vain,
Who formed it to be inhabited:
"I am the LORD, and there is no other.

I have not spoken in secret,
In a dark place of the earth;
I did not say to the seed of Jacob,
'Seek Me in vain';
I, the LORD, speak righteousness,
I declare things that are right.

"Assemble yourselves and come;
Draw near together,
You who have escaped from the nations.
They have no knowledge,
Who carry the wood of their carved image,
And pray to a god that cannot save.
Tell and bring forth your case;
Yes, let them take counsel together.
Who has declared this from ancient time?
Who has told it from that time?
Have not I, the LORD?
And there is no other God besides Me,
A just God and a Savior;
There is none besides Me.

"Look to Me, and be saved,
All you ends of the earth!
For I am God, and there is no other.

I have sworn by Myself;
The word has gone out of My mouth in righteousness,
And shall not return,
That to Me every knee shall bow,
Every tongue shall take an oath.
He shall say, Surely in the LORD I have righteousness
and strength.To Him men shall come,
And all shall be ashamed

Who are incensed against Him.
In the LORD all the descendants of Israel
shall be justified, and shall glory.'"

1 Peter 2:24
who Himself bore our sins in His own body on the tree,
that we, having died to sins, might live for righteousness—
by whose stripes you were healed.

John 4:10
Jesus answered and said to her, "If you knew the gift of God,
and who it is who says to you, 'Give Me a drink,' you would
have asked Him, and He would have given you living water."

1 John 2:2
And He Himself is the propitiation for our sins, and not for
ours only but also for the whole world.

Ephesians 1:7
In Him we have redemption through His blood, the
forgiveness of sins, according to the riches of His grace.

Prayer & Encouragement

Thank You Lord for being You.
There's nobody else like You Lord.

The Work of the Holy Spirit

The Salvation process is carried out in a lost soul by the Holy Spirit. After hearing the Word from a witness, the Holy Spirit, through the Word, makes the truth known that Jesus died to pay the penalty for one's sin and was raised from the dead. This becomes reality in a new convert's heart.

The new convert, now a Christian, believes in
his/her heart and confesses with the mouth that
Jesus is Lord and was raised from the dead.
Romans 10; 1 Corinthians 12:3

As soon as Jesus is accepted and a person is born again. The Holy Spirit enters that person's heart and dwells there (Ezekiel 36:26-27; John 14:15-17; 20:21-22).

Prayer & Encouragement

Thank You Lord for You
Lord, we need Your spirit.

The Role of the Holy Spirit in Our Lives

The Holy Spirit bears us up in our weakness, (Likewise the Spirit also helps in our weaknesses. For we do not know what we should pray for as we ought, but the Spirit Himself makes intercession for us with groanings which cannot be uttered. Now He who searches the hearts knows what the mind of the Spirit is, because He makes intercession for the saints according to the will of God –Romans 8:26-27).

The Holy Spirit aids us in prayer, (But you, beloved, building yourselves up on your most holy faith, praying in the Holy Spirit, -Jude 20; For if I pray in a tongue, my spirit prays, but my understanding is unfruitful 1 Corinthians 14:14).

The Holy Spirit gives us a praising spirit, (but whoever drinks of the water that I shall give him will never thirst. But the water that I shall give him will become in him a fountain of water springing up into everlasting life –John 4:14; On the last day, that great day of the feast, Jesus stood and cried out, saying, "If anyone thirsts, let him come to Me and drink. He who believes in Me, as the Scripture has said, out of his heart will flow rivers of living water." But this He spoke concerning the Spirit, whom those believing[a] in Him would receive; for the Holy Spirit was not yet given, because Jesus was not yet glorified –John 7:37-39).

The Holy Spirit perfects praise, (But when the chief priests and scribes saw the wonderful things that He did, and the children crying out in the temple and saying, "Hosanna to the Son of

David!" they were indignant and said to Him, "Do You hear what these are saying?"

And Jesus said to them, "Yes. Have you never read, 'Out of the mouth of babes and nursing infants You have perfected praise'?" –Matthew 21:15-16.

The Holy Spirit empowers to do miracles, (And these signs will follow those who believe: In My name they will cast out demons; they will speak with new tongues –Mark 16:17).

The Holy Spirit comforts, (And I will pray the Father, and He will give you another Helper, that He may abide with you forever— John 14:16)

The Holy Spirit teaches, (But the Helper, the Holy Spirit, whom the Father will send in My name, He will teach you all things, and bring to your remembrance all things that I said to you –John 14:26).

The Holy Spirit reveals the things of God, (But God has revealed them to us through His Spirit. For the Spirit searches all things, yes, the deep things of God. The natural man does not receive the things of the Spirit of God, for they are foolishness to him; nor can he know them, because they are spiritually discerned -1 Corinthians 2:10, 14).

The Holy Spirit guides into all truths, (I still have many things to say to you, but you cannot bear *them* now. However, when He, the Spirit of truth, has come, He will guide you into all truth; for He will not speak on His own *authority,* but whatever He hears He will speak; and He will tell you things to come –John 16:12-13).

Once saved or born again, determine to receive the Holy Spirit for you shall receive power after the Holy Ghost is come upon you and you shall be witness unto Jesus.
Acts 1:8

Prayer & Encouragement
Thank You Lord for Your Holy Spirit
and all the You do in our lives.

Being Filled with the Holy Ghost

(Ephesians 5:18) or Baptized with the Holy Spirit (John 1:33)

When one gets saved or born again, the Holy Spirit immediately enters his/her heart and dwells there. To be filled with or baptized with the Holy Spirit is a little different. When this happens, God's Holy Spirit endues the person with power to do what God has called that person to do. In most people that get filled with the Holy Spirit, an immediate change is noticed. They are no longer troubled, afraid or sad. Luke 24:51-53 lets us know of this change: Now it came to pass, while He blessed them, that He was parted from them and carried up into heaven. And they worshiped Him, and returned to Jerusalem with great joy, and were continually in the temple praising and blessing God. Amen

Luke 24:49 tells us just before the disciples were blessed, Jesus told them, "Behold, I send the Promise of My Father upon you; but tarry in the city of Jerusalem until you are endued with power from on high." This account is in Acts 1:4-5,8 - And being assembled together with them, He commanded them not to depart from Jerusalem, but to wait for the Promise of the Father, "which," He said, "you have heard from Me; for John truly baptized with water, but you shall be baptized with the Holy Spirit not many days from now... But you shall receive power when the Holy Spirit has come upon you; and you shall be witnesses to Me in Jerusalem, and in all Judea and Samaria, and to the end of the earth."

We need the baptism of the Holy Ghost to carry out the commission from Jesus in Matthew 28:18-20 and Mark 16:15-20. We are taught about these works in John 14:10, 12 (Do you not believe that I am in the Father, and the Father in Me? The words that I speak to you I do not speak on My own *authority;* but the Father who dwells in Me does the works... Most assuredly, I say to you, he who believes in Me, the works that I do he will do also; and greater *works* than these he will do, because I go to My Father). They are the same works Jesus was doing and it would take the same power and anointing of the Holy Spirit He had (Acts 5:12-16; 10:38; Matthew 3:16-17; Luke 4:18-21).

The power first came on the church on the day of Pentecost when Jesus instructed, "But you shall receive power when the Holy Spirit has come upon you; and you shall be witnesses to Me in Jerusalem, and in all Judea and Samaria, and to the end of the earth."-Acts 1:8. The Spirit dwelling within is for fruit bearing (Galatians 5:22-23) as Jesus talked about in John 4:14 (but whoever drinks of the water that I shall give him will never thirst. But the water that I shall give him will become in him a fountain of water springing up into everlasting life). Being filled with or baptized in the Holy Spirit is for service as Jesus indicated in John 7:38-39 (He who believes in Me, as the Scripture has said, out of his heart will flow rivers of living water." [39] But this He spoke concerning the Spirit, whom those believing in Him would receive; for the Holy Spirit was not yet given, because Jesus was not yet glorified).

As new converts believers should be taught to receive the baptism of the Holy Spirit which is evidenced by speaking in other tongues (languages) as the Holy Spirit gives the utterance. Receiving the baptism of the Holy Spirit may happen in several ways which in turn may be narrowed down to two ways...

1. By laying on of hands in prayer (who, when they had come down, prayed for them that they might receive the Holy Spirit. For as yet He had fallen upon none of them. They had only been baptized in the name of the Lord Jesus. Then they laid hands on

them, and they received the Holy Spirit -Acts 8:15-17; he said to them, "Did you receive the Holy Spirit when you believed?" So they said to him, "We have not so much as heard whether there is a Holy Spirit." ... When they heard this, they were baptized in the name of the Lord Jesus. And when Paul had laid hands on them, the Holy Spirit came upon them, and they spoke with tongues and prophesied. -Acts 19:2, 5-6).

2. By faith (While Peter was still speaking these words, the Holy Spirit fell upon all those who heard the word. And those of the circumcision who believed were astonished, as many as came with Peter, because the gift of the Holy Spirit had been poured out on the Gentiles also. For they heard them speak with tongues and magnify God. Then Peter answered, "Can anyone forbid water, that these should not be baptized who have received the Holy Spirit just as we *have?*" And he commanded them to be baptized in the name of the Lord. Then they asked him to stay a few days -Acts 10:44-48; That the blessing of Abraham might come upon the Gentiles in Christ Jesus, that we might receive the promise of the Spirit through faith -Gal. 3:14).

God's Salvation Plan
Soul Winning Tools (The Word)

The fruit of the righteous is a tree of life,
And he who wins souls is wise.
– Proverbs 11:30

EVERYONE ON THIS EARTH IS A SINNER

As it is written:

Romans 3:10-12, 3:23
"There is none righteous, no, not one;
There is none who understands;
There is none who seeks after God.
They have all turned aside;
They have together become unprofitable;
There is none who does good, no, not one …

For all have sinned and fall short of the glory of God"

Psalm 14:2-3
The LORD looks down from heaven upon the children of men,
To see if there are any who understand, who seek God.
They have all turned aside,
They have together become corrupt;
There is none who does good,
No, not one.

1 John 1:8, 10
If we say that we have no sin, we deceive ourselves, and the
truth is not in us … If we say that we have not sinned, we
make Him a liar, and His word is not in us

<u>1 Kings 8:46</u>
"When they sin against You (for there is no one who does not sin), and You become angry with them and deliver them to the enemy, and they take them captive to the land of the enemy, far or near;

<u>Psalm 130:8</u>
And He shall redeem Israel
From all his iniquities

Prayer & Encouragement

Lord, help me to be a soul winner. Help me to "Think Souls".
Help me to let my light so shine that men, women,
boys and girls Will ask how can I make
Jesus the Lord of my life?

Your Word never goes out void.
You Lord will accomplish Your plan
and Your purpose as we minister
Your Word and share with others

The Penalty for Sin/the Punishment for Unbelief

Romans 6:23.
For the wages of sin is death, but the gift of God is eternal life in Christ Jesus our Lord.

John 3:18, 36
"He who believes in Him is not condemned; but he who does not believe is condemned already, because he has not believed in the name of the only begotten Son of God ... He who believes in the Son has everlasting life; and he who does not believe the Son shall not see life, but the wrath of God abides on him."

John 8:24, 34
Therefore I said to you that you will die in your sins; for if you do not believe that I am *He,* you will die in your sins ... Jesus answered them, "Most assuredly, I say to you, whoever commits sin is a slave of sin.

Galatians 3:10
For as many as are of the works of the law are under the curse; for it is written, "Cursed is everyone who does not continue in all things which are written in the book of the law, to do them."

Isaiah 57:20-21
But the wicked are like the troubled sea.
When it cannot rest, Whose waters cast up mire and dirt.
"There is no peace," Says my God, "for the wicked."

2 Thessalonians 1:7-9
And to give you who are troubled rest with us when the Lord Jesus is revealed from heaven with His mighty angels, in flaming fire taking vengeance on those who do not know God, and on those who do not obey the gospel of our Lord Jesus Christ. These shall be punished with everlasting destruction from the presence of the Lord and from the glory of His power,

Revelation 21:8
But the cowardly, unbelieving, abominable, murderers, sexually immoral, sorcerers, idolaters, and all liars shall have their part in the lake which burns with fire and brimstone, which is the second death."

Hebrews 10:28-29
Anyone who has rejected Moses' law dies without mercy on the testimony of two or three witnesses. [29] Of how much worse punishment, do you suppose, will he be thought worthy who has trampled the Son of God underfoot, counted the blood of the covenant by which he was sanctified a common thing, and insulted the Spirit of grace?

Prayer & Encouragement
Lord, touch hearts as they read Your Word.
Yes Lord You are The Living Word.
You Lord make the difference in our lives.

GOD'S LOVE, MERCY, AND GRACE

<u>John 3:16</u>
For God so loved the world that He gave His only begotten
Son, that whoever believes in Him should not perish but have
everlasting life.

<u>Romans 5:6-11</u>
For when we were still without strength, in due time Christ
died for the ungodly. For scarcely for a righteous man will
one die; yet perhaps for a good man someone would even
dare to die. But God demonstrates His own love toward us,
in that while we were still sinners, Christ died for us. Much
more then, having now been justified by His blood, we shall
be saved from wrath through Him. For if when we were
enemies we were reconciled to God through the death of His
Son, much more, having been reconciled, we shall be saved
by His life. And not only that, but we also rejoice in God
through our Lord Jesus Christ, through whom we have now
received the reconciliation.

<u>Isaiah 53:5-6</u>
But He was wounded for our transgressions,
He was bruised for our iniquities;
The chastisement for our peace was upon Him,
And by His stripes we are healed.
All we like sheep have gone astray.
We have turned, every one, to his own way;
And the LORD has laid on Him the iniquity of us all.

<u>John 10:10</u>
The thief does not come except to steal, and to kill, and to destroy. I have come that they may have life, and that they may have *it* more abundantly.

<u>Galatians 3:3</u>
Are you so foolish? Having begun in the Spirit, are you now being made perfect by the flesh?

<u>1 Peter 1:18-19</u>
Knowing that you were not redeemed with corruptible things, like silver or gold, from your aimless conduct received by tradition from your fathers, but with the precious blood of Christ, as of a lamb without blemish and without spot.

<u>Ephesians 2:8</u>
For by grace you have been saved through faith, and that not of yourselves; it is the gift of God.

Prayer & Encouragement

Thank You Lord for Your love, grace and mercy.
If it had not been for You on my side Lord where would I be?
Lord, I can never thank You enough!!!

God's love, grace and mercy towards us are
amazing and mind blowing. Totally awesome!!!!

JESUS OUR RISEN SAVIOR AND ETERNAL INTERCESSOR

1 Corinthians 15:1-4
Moreover, brethren, I declare to you the gospel which I preached to you, which also you received and in which you stand, by which also you are saved, if you hold fast that word which I preached to you—unless you believed in vain.

For I delivered to you first of all that which I also received: that Christ died for our sins according to the Scriptures, and that He was buried, and that He rose again the third day according to the Scriptures,

Jude 1:24-25
Now to Him who is able to keep you from stumbling, And to present you faultless Before the presence of His glory with exceeding joy,

Romans 8:34
Who is he who condemns? It is Christ who died, and furthermore is also risen, who is even at the right hand of God, who also makes intercession for us.

John 1:12
But as many as received Him, to them He gave the right to become children of God, to those who believe in His name.

Acts 16:31
So they said, "Believe on the Lord Jesus Christ, and you will be saved, you and your household."

John 3:16
For God so loved the world that He gave His only begotten
Son, that whoever believes in Him should
not perish but have everlasting life.

Isaiah 45:22
"Look to Me, and be saved,
All you ends of the earth!
For I am God, and there is no other.

Romans 10:9-10
That if you confess with your mouth the Lord Jesus and
believe in your heart that God has raised Him from the dead,
you will be saved. For with the heart one believes unto
righteousness, and with the mouth confession
is made unto salvation.

Acts 10:43
To Him all the Prophets witness that, through His name,
whoever believes in Him will receive remission of sins."

Acts 13:39
And by Him everyone who believes is justified
from all things from which you could not
be justified by the law of Moses.

The Intercessor

1 John 2:1
My little children, these things I write to you, so that you may not sin. And if anyone sins, we have an Advocate with the Father, Jesus Christ the righteous.

Hebrews 7:25
Therefore He is also able to save to the uttermost those who come to God through Him, since He always lives to make intercession for them.

Prayer & Encouragement

Thank You Lord for standing in the gap for me. Thank You for taking my place and pleading my case with the Father. Thank You for Your blood Lord which washes away my sins.

Thank You Lord that when I confessed with my mouth and believed in my heart that Father God raised You from the dead I accepted salvation as a free gift. I am saved.

Elder Vivian Mackey-Johnson is a PK (preacher's kid). Growing up as a pastor's child, she learned a lot about ministry. She gave her life to the Lord during a Youth for Christ Crusade at the age of sixteen years old on July 16, 1979. She is a preacher of the gospel. She has served in many leadership capacities in the church, such as missionary, teacher, praise and worship leader, choir director, church clerk, church trustee, and assistant superintendent of the church school.

Elder Vivian worked as a graphic designer for nineteen years at a major newspaper. Today she is a licensed sales agent for health insurance and ministers to seniors. Elder Vivian is a loving wife, mother, and grandmother. She resides in Florida with her husband, Elder Moses Johnson Sr., and son Moses Johnson Jr.

Elder Moses Johnson Sr. has been a Christian since October 17, 1979. He gave his life to the Lord during an open-air crusade in Kingston, Jamaica. He became a member of the Church of God of Prophecy at Maxfield Ave., Kingston, Jamaica.

After attending the University of the West Indies and University of Technology, both in St. Andrew, Jamaica, and Virginia Union University Theological Seminary satellite classes at the EBA School of Religion in New York State, Moses was ordained a minister in Mt. Sinai Baptist Church Cathedral. Elder Moses also taught remedial English and engineering science at Tivoli Garden High School in Kingston, Jamaica, and integrated science at Roosevelt Junior High School in Roosevelt, New York.

Elder Moses resides with his wife, Elder Vivian, and son Moses Jr. in Orlando, Florida.